DESPOTISM AND
DIFFERENTIAL REPRODUCTION
A Darwinian View of History

DESPOTISM AND DIFFERENTIAL REPRODUCTION
A Darwinian View of History

Laura L. Betzig

ALDINE
Publishing Company
New York

ABOUT THE AUTHOR
Laura L. Betzig is currently affiliated with the Museum of Zoology, University of Michigan. Dr. Betzig has authored many scholarly articles and is currently co-editor of (with Monique Borgerhoff Mulder and Paul Turke) *Human Reproductive Behaviour: A Darwinian Perspective.* She is also involved in an extensive research project in Micronesia.

Aldine Publishing Company
200 Saw Mill River Road
Hawthorne, New York 10532

Library of Congress Cataloging-in-Publication Data

Betzig, L. L. (Laura L.) 1953–
  Despotism and differential reproduction.

  Bibliography: p.
  1. Despotism—Cross-cultural studies. 2. Human
reproduction—Social aspects—Cross-cultural studies.
3. Polygamy—Cross-cultural studies. 4. Sociobiology.
5. Darwin, Charles, 1809–1882. I. Title
GN492.7.B47   1986
ISBN 0-202-01171-2   304.6′3   85-20010

Printed in the United States of America
10 9 8 7 6 5 4 3 2 1

FOR MY FATHER AND MOTHER

CONTENTS

> Much light will be thrown on the origin of man and his history.
>
> —Darwin (1859:573)

PREFACE

Darwin ended his *Origin of Species* with that prophecy. It has since provoked, like many, a flood of argument and a trickle of evidence. In the first century after the *Origin of Species*, virtually no one tested Darwin's theory against the evidence of human history. In the last decade, that tide has changed; this book is caught up in it. It tests the proposition that the evolved end of human life is its reproduction, against the literature on conflict resolution from over a hundred societies across space and time. And the results, like much of what has been done in the past ten years, seem to me both surprisingly and convincingly uphold Darwin's prophecy. Light seems in fact to have been shed on human political and reproductive history.

Certainly, over the past ten years, and probably over the last hundred, a lot more has been said about why questions about how human history has been shaped by natural history should not be asked, than has been said in an effort to answer them. Unfortunately, some of the most respected contributors to both evolutionary theory and to the evidence from history and ethnography are among those objecting to testing Darwinian hypotheses about human society. The salient reason seems to be one common to every field of investigation: the findings might be misused. My counter is as common: they might, on the other hand, be used to the general good. A basic premise behind any research has been that an understanding of the way things *are* should contribute to our ability to change them to the way we would like them to *be*. I believe that this premise has often been justified. And I believe that it is likely to be justified in this case, or I would not have written the book. Among the most repetitive aspects of human history has been the exploitation of power. The results here bear that redundancy out. In

ix

some way, I hope that an understanding of what historical and natural historical conditions have promoted despotism might contribute to its eradication.

A number of men and women, who probably share my feelings about despotism, have helped over the past five years to produce this book. My debt in any Darwinian work is first to Richard D. Alexander, whose instruction, encouragement, and support of his students offers one of the few good demonstrations of his own contention that an understanding of natural history may afford a change of course. Whatever is best in my work derives from his introduction to and direction in Darwinian theory.

My dissertation advisors, Napoleon Chagnon and William Irons, pioneered the test of that theory with human behavioral fact. To Chagnon I owe the obvious, outstanding precedent of an evolutionary analysis of political behavior, the incentive of criticism, and many encouraging words. To Irons I owe the first formal correlation between the means and ends of reproductive success, repeated reminders to test alternative hypotheses, and, most immediately, the midwifing of this study of despotism and differential reproduction. He has since had the genial patience to suffer through more versions of it than anyone else.

To Malcolm Dow I owe a borrowed sophistication about cross-cultural sampling and statistical techniques. Having made his reputation, in part, by working out a mathematical solution to Galton's problem, he was the best man I could have found to impart, with a lot of affable argument, such advice.

Over the years, I have had the pleasure of the company of a Darwinian sherry-sipping cohort, including Nancy Berté, Monique Borgerhoff Mulder, Mark Flinn, Joe Manson, and Paul Turke, whose conversation undoubtedly has been to our mutual betterment. Readers of various drafts of this project, including Robert Boyd, Jesse Chanley, Ronald Cohen, Bobbi Low, Ann McGuire, Gene Mesher, Randy Nesse, Beverly Strassmann, Pierre van den Berghe, Richard Wrangham, all of the above, and especially Mildred Dickemann, have contributed to the result. Dr. Dickemann's work, more than any other, has been a model for my own; her applications of Darwinian theory to the ethnographic and historical record have been among the most exciting done. More particularly, she took the time to go through every page of a penultimate draft; her characteristically excellent criticism has improved the final version.

Thanks to Northwestern University for a Graduate Dissertation Research Grant which made possible a trip to the Cumulative Cross Cultural Coding Center at the University of Pittsburgh, to John Saffirio for arranging for a place to stay, and to Jack Roberts and Steve Gaulin for allowing an unknown privileged access to the standard cross-cultural sample materials there. Greg Williams, Mies van der Rohe's emissary to Darwinian sippers of sherry, beautifully adapted Murdock and White's standard sample maps.

Richard Wrangham has seemed to share my enthusiasm about this study since soon after its inception. Without his generous encouragement, it might not have gone to press; without his careful editorship, it would not have made as good a book.

Last, but not least, thanks for the bare essentials of personal maintenance go to my parents, who have by now contributed in good faith for more than thirty years, and to Paul Turke, who has recently and ably assumed the increasing weight of that responsibility.

Laura L. Betzig

> And lest there should be any doubt upon a matter, which does not in the least concern science, I may add that, being a man myself, I have never had the least doubt as to the importance of the human race, of their mental and moral characteristics . . . . The supreme value which, I feel, ought to be attached to these several aspects of human excellence, appears to provide no good reason for asserting, as is sometimes done, with a petulant indignation not unmixed with spiritual arrogance, that such a low matter as natural causation cannot be of importance to these sublime things. On the contrary, it introduces the strongest motive for striving to know, as accurately and distinctly as possible, in what ways natural causes have acted in their evolutionary upbuilding. . . .
> —Sir Ronald Fisher (1958:190)

1

INTRODUCTION

Over the course of history, a lot of people have lost their heads. If the "Secret History" (Procopius, 550), for instance, is to be believed, the Byzantine emperor Justinian did what he could to lend the word despotism its uncharitable connotation. A litany of attributions includes: Within days of coming to power, he executed the head of the palace eunuchs for making an "injudicious remark" against an archpriest; he accused a member of the opposition faction of committing "offenses against boys," and had him dismembered, for an uncomplementary attitude toward the empress Theodora; and he took immense wealth from the grandson of a former emperor when a will openly rumored false was produced upon his "unexpected" death. Procopius suggests that these sorts of accusations, punishments, and false documents were liberally brought against members of the other party, against anybody "who happened to have come up against the rulers in some other way," and, especially, against those exceptionally well off.

Justinian's subjects seem to have done what they could to resist: they risked great cost in raising the Nika revolt, and lost. In January of 532

AD, members of both Byzantine factions, peasants ruined by taxation and forced to emigrate to Byzantium, and members of the senatorial ranks set fire to the city, held the palace in a virtual state of siege, and crowned another emperor. Justinian's great general, Belisarius, killed the insurrection, and in the process, over 30,000 men and women (Bury, 1923). The emperor ruled for another 33 years, his will apparently as strong as the force that had successfully backed it up. Contrary to relatively republican precedent, but consistent with an Oriental trend, he and Theodora eventually asked subjects to prostrate themselves flat on their faces in front of them, kiss one of each of their feet, and address them as "*despotes*" and "*despoina*," master and mistress, making themselves, by implication, their slaves.

The "despotism" of Theodora and Justinian makes a good etymological beginning; but even it is, of course, hardly a chronological one. The arbitrary extent of their authority was neither unprecedented nor unsurpassed. Despotism, defined here as the exercised right of heads of societies to murder their subjects arbitrarily and with impunity, is in evidence in the first Old and New World states, and is a long way from being eradicated in the twentieth century.

Lord Acton once pointed out that "absolute power corrupts absolutely" (1948:364), surprising hardly anyone. The perhaps naive question asked here is, *why?* The answer investigated follows from Darwin. If men and women are products of natural selection, then the evolved end of their existence should be essentially, very simply, the production of children, grandchildren, and other nondescendant kinsmen.

Innocuous as this might sound at first, the implications unfortuately are not. Although a very modest share of resources might enable one to live reasonably comfortably, his share, as Malthus (1798) pointed out, must increase proportionately with the size of his family. If every individual provides for as many descendants as possible, competition is inevitable. The important result, as Darwin pointed out, must be that winners leave the legacy of whatever heritable traits helped in that competition to their children. Among Darwin's (1859) own examples: high browsing giraffes should have evolved long necks (p. 161); orchids should have evolved their spout-shaped lower lips in order to get pollinated (p. 142); cuckoos should have evolved to lay eggs in other birds' nests (p. 190).

And men and women should have evolved to seek out positions of strength as a *means* to reproduction. Power, prestige, and privileged access to resources should be sought, not as ends in themselves, but as prerequisites to procreation. A lease to use power to serve one's own interests should translate into the production of children and grandchildren. Despotism should be expected to coincide with differential reproduction.

Such a theory *by no means* is meant to imply a justification! Nor is it meant to suggest that despotism, or having great numbers of children, or anything else for that matter, even if they have been under some circumstances adaptive strategies, are under any circumstances inevitable. If, in fact, this or any other theory makes possible an understanding of human actions, and of the circumstances which prompt their manifestation and suppression, it might even make it possible to change them. The laws of nature often have little in common with the way we would have them. But as Fisher (1958:190), and many others, have stressed, our ability to understand them must often precede our ability to overcome them.

The Darwinian hypothesis that power is exploited to the end of reproduction is tested here according to the following plan. First, an often stunning mass of ethnographic and historical facts from a sample of over a hundred world societies is recounted to show whether or not, and how, as a rule, men and women have abused their power to bias the resolution of conflicts in their own interests. Then, a colorful literature of a completely different sort details the means successful men may have taken advantage of in order to make children.

Such an extraordinarily simple explanation as Darwin's, that power has been exploited to the end of reproduction, has, of course, been antedated by a number of widely respected, often much more complicated alternatives. A great many, addressed either to conflict resolution and political exploitation, or to polygyny and other reproductive strategies, have stood up against both the evidence and time. No explanation would be at all tenable without careful consideration of them. The outstanding theories of polygyny, comparative law, and, especially, Marxism, are evaluated here in conjunction with the evidence, and in comparison with a Darwinian interpretation.

W. B. Yeats, in his poem, "Sailing to Byzantium," was distressed at being an old man among the "fish, flesh, and fowl" procreating all around him in Ireland, and willed himself to what he perceived as the more two-dimensional ideal of an immortal, immaterial Byzantine world. But, if Darwin was right, ludicrous as it might sound, Yeats might have been wrong. Byzantine birds of hammered gold "set upon a golden bough to sing/of what is past, and passing, and to come" might have made a music at least as sensual as what Yeats heard a thousand years later and more than a thousand miles away. And it might have seemed especially so to old men, like Justinian, who had the power to have it made.

What follows is, broadly, an attempt to determine how much light a

Darwinian theory of evolved motivation sheds on the problem of human competition. It is, in short, an attempt to determine how often power has been used to the end of reproduction, not just in Byzantium, but throughout the course of history and before. To start, the theory must be more fully fleshed out.

DARWINIAN THEORY

Natural Selection

His theory seemed to Darwin to shed such light on the phenomena of nature that he wrote, "Nothing is easier than to admit in words the truth of the universal struggle for life, or more difficult—at least I have found it so—than constantly to bear this conclusion in mind. Yet unless it be thoroughly engrained in the mind, the whole economy of nature, with every fact on distribution, rarity, abundance, extinctions and variation, will be dimly seen or quite misunderstood" (1859:52).

In 1859, he published his conclusion that wherever more individuals are produced than can survive, a struggle for existence must ensue in which the best adapted most successfully propagate their kind. He called this process natural selection. Put simply, the theory states that *heritable traits which promote reproduction will spread*. Descendants of those who most successfully reproduced should, in turn, manifest the cumulative legacy of their ancestors' traits. Darwin devoted a lifetime to the demonstration that the theory of natural selection may afford an explanation of such diverse phenomena as the extraordinary length of giraffes' necks, orchid flowering and pollination, and parts of the neural morphologies and behavioral repertoires of cuckoos, wasps, house cats, and men.

It is important that, in his discussion of natural selection, Darwin concluded that the struggle to survive and reproduce "will almost invariably be most severe between individuals of the same species" (1859:60; cf., e.g., Darwin 1871:483). This conclusion makes possible the specific, *falsifiable* prediction that traits promoting reproduction and reproductive competition should show up in individual organisms, rather than groups. Generally, where there are not enough resources to allow those dependent upon them to reproduce to the greatest possible extent, *evolved* individual interests must be expected to conflict. Following a generation-long controversy on the problem of the "unit of selection," this conclusion now represents a consensus among contemporary Darwinian theorists (e.g., Alexander and Borgia, 1978; Dawkins, 1976, 1982; Fisher, 1958:49; Lewontin, 1970; Wade, 1978; Williams and Williams, 1957; Williams, 1966; Wilson, 1980; Wright, 1945, 1980).

The prediction that, under almost all conditions, individuals should have evolved to compete over reproductive ends, does not, however, preclude the possibility of their cooperation. In social species, apparent altruism among individuals may contribute to their own fertility either as reciprocity or as nepotism.

NEPOTISM The idea that related individuals might share an evolved interest in one another's welfare has had a long history in biological theory. In discussing the "social instincts," meant to bind individuals to one another, Darwin included family ties (1871:912). Fisher (1930), in developing the concept of reproductive value, suggested that "there will also, no doubt, be indirect effects in cases in which an animal favours or impedes the survival or reproduction of its relatives" (p. 27). He also suggested that mimicry (p. 178), and heroism, a trait tending its bearers toward "an increased probability of entering an occupation not easily to be reconciled with family life," could be selected for, given that sufficient reproductive compensation could be conferred upon surviving kin (p. 265). Haldane (1932) discussed the possibility of the evolution of a trait causing a person to risk his life for his child. In addition, the evolution of sterility in the social insects has been explained by Darwin (1859), Fisher (1930), Haldane (1932), and Williams and Williams (1957), as well as by Hamilton (1964), as offset by contributions of such individuals to reproduction of family members.

Hamilton, in 1963 and 1964, made explicit the prediction that an individual should be willing to take on a reproductive cost to himself where such an action results in a big enough reproductive payoff to a genetic relative (see also, e.g., West Eberhard, 1975; Abugov and Michod, 1981). Specifically, he argued that "the social behavior of a species evolves in such a way that in each distinct behavior-evoking situation the individual will seem to value his neighbor's fitness against his own according to the coefficients of relationship appropriate to that situation" (1964:20). Hamilton calls such nepotistic behavior "inclusive fitness maximization"; it also has been referred to as "kin selection" (Maynard Smith, 1964).

RECIPROCITY. In his discussion of the "moral sense," Darwin (1871) was concerned with the emotions which cause people to want to be liked and to avoid being disliked. He suggested that a man might occasionally act in his own interests, even when they are at odds with others', but that "he will be conscious that if his conduct were known to his fellows, it would meet with their disapprobation; and few are so destitute of sympathy as not to feel discomfort when this is realised" (p. 486). Darwin argued that as reasoning powers and foresight improved, "each man would soon learn that if he aided his fellow men, he would commonly receive aid in return. From this low motive he might acquire the habit of aiding his fellows" (p. 499). Williams (1966), citing Darwin, has said that he sees no reason why a conscious motive is necessary; natural selection should favor giving help to others as long as it is reciprocated occasionally, consciously or not (p. 94).

Trivers (1971) specifically formulated the idea of what he called "reciprocal altruism." He argued that while random dispensation of altruism by individuals could not be favored by selection, its nonrandom dispensation by reference to genetic relationship (Hamilton's inclusive fitness effect), or the probability of future reciprocity (reciprocal altruism), could be selected for. He pointed out that reciprocal altruism would most likely occur when individuals involved interacted repeatedly, were afforded many opportunities to benefit by being recipients of altruistic acts, and were able to render roughly equivalent benefits to each other at roughly equivalent costs. He also argued that many human emotions, such as friendship, liking and disliking, and guilt, may serve to regulate the individual's dispensation of altruism.

More recently, West Eberhard (1978) and Wrangham (1982) have pointed out that cases of essentially simultaneous benefit may be conceived of as mutualism; and Moore (1984) has suggested that, in many instances, apparent altruism may actually result because the cost of *not* giving up a benefit is great. Axelrod and Hamilton (1981; Axelrod, 1984) have further developed reciprocity theory by soliciting strategies from scholars and playing them off against one another; a "tit for tat" pattern won. Finally, Alexander (1979; 1985) has often stressed the importance in human societies of both direct and indirect reciprocity, the first coming from the recipient of the original altruistic act, the latter including rewards coming from society at large, or from other than the initial recipient. He has suggested that reciprocity should be most direct in brief encounters by individuals unlikely to engage in future interactions, while indirect reciprocity should bind groups of individuals involved in long-term relationships (cf. Sahlins, 1972; Alexander, 1975). The significance of reciprocity in human society has not, of course, gone unnoticed by social theorists. Outstanding examples in anthropology include Mauss (1925), Malinowski (1922, 1926), and Levi-Strauss (1949).

To sum up, Darwinian theory makes the simple prediction that men and women *will* cooperate when it is in their reproductive interests to do so. Where, however, genealogical kinship and reciprocity are absent, individual conflicts of interest are expected to exist. To the extent that individual interests are not overridden by common interest, then, individuals should have evolved to exploit positions of strength to the end of maximizing their own reproductive success, even at the expense of others. The means to that end may differ, however, according to a number of circumstances. One of the most important of these is sex.

Sexual Selection

Darwin proposed a special kind of selection to account for evolved adapations specific to females and males. He suggested that, by sexual selection, individuals having "weapons" with which to defeat competitors for a mate, or "charms" with which to attract one, might leave the most progeny (1871). Darwin noted that, very generally, males appear to pursue females sexually, while females as generally appear to be coy. He guessed that bias might have something to do with the fact that "the female has to spend much more organic matter in formation of her ova, whereas the male expends much force in fierce contests with his rivals" (1871:581). Overall, he argued, the expenditure of matter and effort by either sex was probably roughly the same, although effected along different routes, and at different rates.

Bateman, in 1948, argued that, most often being the lesser physiological investors in progeny, males are in a better position than females to gain reproductively by multiple matings. By this difference he accounted for the apparent general tendency of males toward promiscuity, and for the comparable female tendency toward caution and discrimination in mating. As Williams (1966) showed, Bateman's rule is substantiated by the exceptions: in species in which males, after conception, assume the greater share of parental care, the associated behavior patterns are switched as well. Females assume the aggressive role in courtship and tend toward promiscuity; males are reserved in courtship and mating (see an excellent review of the evidence on this subject in Daly and Wilson, 1983:156-163).

Strategies males and females employ to the end of reproducing are, then, predicted to differ to the extent that the difference in investment patterns, which defines sex difference, exists (Trivers, 1972). Males generally invest less in each offspring, and therefore have the physiological ability to produce more. Given an evolved fifty-fifty sex ratio (see Fisher, 1930), males are therefore in a position to compete with one another for reproductive opportunities, and females are in a position to choose among competing males (Bateman, 1948; Trivers, 1972). Depending on her reproductive requirements, a female may be expected to opt among available males for some mix of ability to contribute parental care and heritable ability to father reproductively successful progeny (see Fisher, 1930; Orians, 1969; Hamilton and Zuk, 1982; reviews in Borgia, 1979; Bateson, 1983; Irons, 1983).

One more important point: to the extent that they do benefit reproductively by helping to care themselves for progeny, males must be strongly selected to take up an additional strategy. They must take care to ensure that offspring they care for are theirs: they must defend against cuckoldry (Trivers, 1972; Dickemann, 1981).

Women, of course, contribute substantially more physiologically to the investment in children than do men. All of these predictions, therefore, hold for humans. Reproductive rewards sought by men and women able to resolve conflicts in their own interests may, then, be expected to differ as follows. Men may be expected to benefit by reproductive access to as many healthy, fertile women as they can successfully impregnate (and possibly even more if only to keep reproductive competitors from having access to them), by obtaining the resources necessary to obtain and support them and their children, and by endeavoring to keep them cloistered against other fertile men. Women may be expected to seek men with whatever heritable traits are apparently most likely to produce reproductively successful children, with sufficient power and wealth to defend and support them, and, at best, with the ability to bequeath to sons the means to reproduce polygynously.

Two Points of Clarification

MEASURING FITNESS. In the evolutionary long run, the end of all such strategies must be the reproductive success of individual genes. However, fitness, or the rate of spread of any given gene, is itself virtually unmeasurable (Wright, 1968). Its measurement must be approximate. Mating success, lifetime reproductive success, and number of descendants in any given generation have been used as fitness approximations of increasing depth in time, and therefore accuracy (Dunbar, 1982). The present study deals with only the first, number of wives and concubines held simultaneously by the head of a hierarchy. It is the best estimate the historical record affords. Given the magnitude of variation in the number of women conjugally related to heads of social groups, and the significant fact that both power and polygyny are increasingly often bequeathed to lineal descendants as harems increase in size, this measure should afford a strong indication of the spread of genes in descendant generations, that is, a good approximation of fitness.

DISTINGUISHING PROXIMATE FROM ULTIMATE. Again, in the evolutionary long run, natural selection should produce individuals who behave in order to maximize the spread of their genes. This end has been referred to as the "ultimate" cause of individuals' actions, and has been distinguished from the more immediate means by which such a long-term end is effected, or "proximate" causes (discussed in Mayr,

1961; Tinbergen, 1963; Daly and Wilson, 1983). Uncertainty about the interface between the two may in part be responsible for assumptions that Darwinian explanations of human behavior constitute a simplistic form of biological determinism (e.g., Gould, 1980), in which behaviors are supposed to be mapped directly onto genes without any ontogenetic input. In fact, of course, biology is always prerequisite to behavior; in some sense, the actions of every organism, including men and women, must be genetically "determined."

A complex of basic human emotional responses including, for example, a masculine enjoyment of sexual variety (Symons, 1979), sexual jealousy (Daly, Wilson, and Weghorst, 1982), closeness of feeling among children reared in close association (Westermarck, 1891; Spiro, 1958; Shepher, 1971), and, especially, a very strong affection for children and grandchildren, each realized to the variable extent that context permits, may in large part be adequate to prompt, for example, polygyny, the claustration of women, and nepotism. These "proximate," in this case psychological, mechanisms, might have been designed by natural selection, to be produced by the interaction of genes with predictable environments. They may be among the most important affecting a number of simple and complex behaviors contributing to successful reproduction (cf. Symons, 1979).

It is essential to point out again that an understanding of the "proximate" or "ultimate" function of human action is absolutely not meant to justify its perpetration. It is meant, in Symons' (1979) phrase, to be descriptive, not prescriptive. As Alexander (1979; 1985) has probably most frequently argued, an understanding of the "ultimate" function of human behaviors, of their "proximate" mechanisms, and of the conditions under which they are manifested, may be a sound basis for undoing them.

HYPOTHESES

Darwinian theory predicts that to the extent that conflicts of interest among individuals are not overridden by common interest, or by an overpowering force, they will be manifested (Alexander and Borgia, 1978), and they will, ultimately, be reproductively motivated. Where such conflicts exist, men and women are expected to exploit positions of strength in resolving them to their own advantage; and they are expected to turn that advantage to proportionate means to reproduction. Hierarchical power should predict a biased outcome in conflict resolution, which should in turn predict size of the winner's harem, for men, a measure of success in reproduction.

The alternatives to the Darwinian hypothesis must be either that natural selection in humans has been most important at some level other than the individual (see versions of this statement in Darwin, 1859; Williams, 1966; Alexander, 1979; Dunbar, 1982), or that culture or god has exonerated individuals from evolved biological constraints to such an extent that human behavior is no longer predictable in those terms (a very small sampling of recent, explicit variations on this theme includes Sahlins, 1976a; Dawkins, 1976, 1982; Durham, 1979, 1982; Pulliam and Dunford, 1980; Boyd and Richerson, 1982; and Chen, Cavalli-Sforza, and Feldman, 1982; contrast Alexander, 1979; Daly, 1982; Flinn and Alexander, 1982; Turke, 1984a). Deistic alternatives, i.e., that a higher power has intervened to sway natural events from the predicted course, are of course the most immediate with which Darwin himself was concerned (1859, 1871).

Again, a number of time-honored theories other than Darwin's have been proposed to account for both polygyny and despotism. Each of them to a greater or lesser extent tacitly assumes that one of the above alternatives is true: that individual selection has not been the predominant force in human evolution, or more often, that human action has been unbound from biological constraints. None of these theories has, however, explicitly predicted that despotism and differential reproduction should coincide. Alternative theories of conflict resolution and the exploitation of power, including Marxism, and theories advanced to explain polygyny, are both profuse and complex. They, and their relationships to Darwinism, will be discussed in conjunction with the evidence in conclusion to the chapters on despotism and differential reproduction.

METHODS

Appropriately enough, these hypotheses were tested by the Darwinian, or comparative, method (Ghieselin, 1969). Data on hierarchy, despotism, and polygyny were amassed on a representative sample of the world's societies. The most widely used sample in cross-cultural research is currently the standard cross-cultural sample developed by Murdock and White (1969), consisting of 186 societies pinpointed in space and time. These societies include, however, a substantial number in which the resolution of ingroup conflicts is not determined autonomously, but, for example, by a colonial authority. Tuden and Marshall (1972) have coded each of these societies for degree of political autonomy. Only the 106 groups of the Murdock-White sample which Tuden and Marshall coded as either fully autonomous or enjoying de facto autonomy were included in the present study. Of these, two societies, the Ajie, for which all available sources were in foreign languages, and

Mao, for which the single available English language source provided insufficient information, were dropped. The present study, therefore, is based on a sample of 104 societies. Specific information concerning the pinpointing of each in time and space by Murdock and White is listed in Appendix I. Figures 1.1 through 1.6 locate each society on one of six world region maps, also adapted from Murdock and White (1969).

In collecting information concerning polygyny and conflict resolution, both the original ethnographic data indexed in the Human Relations Area Files (HRAF), and ethnographic sources not in the HRAF, were used. Sources used included those listed in bibliographies published in *Ethnology* in a series of papers with standard cross-cultural sample codes (Murdock and Morrow, 1970; Barry and Paxson, 1971; Murdock and Wilson, 1972; Tuden and Marshall, 1972; Murdock and Provost, 1973; Barry, Josephson, Lauer, and Marshall, 1976; Broude and Greene, 1976). Information about the number of levels in a society's jurisdictional hierarchy had already been coded by Murdock and Provost (1973) for standard sample societies. Each of these variables is defined specifically in Appendix II.

The chapters that follow spell out the results. They determine, first, how consistently *does* exploitation parallel power? Second, how often does a demonstrated ability to win conflicts of interest translate into reproductive success? The next three chapters flesh out such conclusions with the often striking ethnographic and historical evidence. In order to avoid accusations of "advocacy" (Wilson, 1975), the societies reviewed have been restricted to those pinpointed in the present sample. Each of these chapters is followed by or interspersed with theoretical conclusions. Chapter 5 is made up of a longhand and statistical summary; and Chapter 6 offers a discussion of the conditions which might have given rise to despotism, differential reproduction, and, eventually, democracy.

Before beginning a discussion of the rise, and fall, of despotism and differential reproduction, an important caveat bears repetition. Much of anthropology seems to have been devoted to an argument that man in the state of nature is an egalitarian being (e.g., Engels, 1884; a lengthy discussion follows), with the implication that his evident capacity to become otherwise is learned, and so can be unlearned. This, without doubt, has been done with noble intention. However, the demonstrated capacity of individuals to be more or less equal in society *speaks for itself*. Again, the ends of evolution exist as fact; our ability to use them to effect ends of positive or negative *value* by altering the conditions under which they must be expressed may depend upon our understanding of them as ends of evolution (Alexander, 1979).

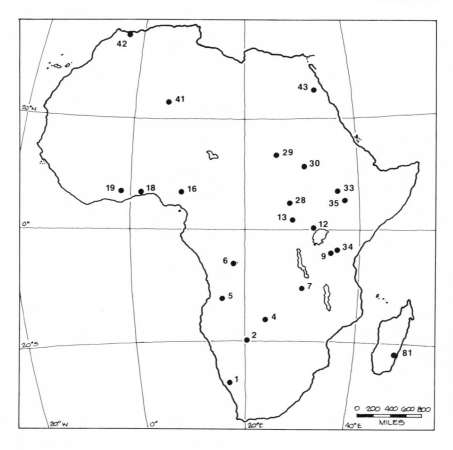

Figure 1.1 Africa. Numbers on map refer to those given in Appendix I.

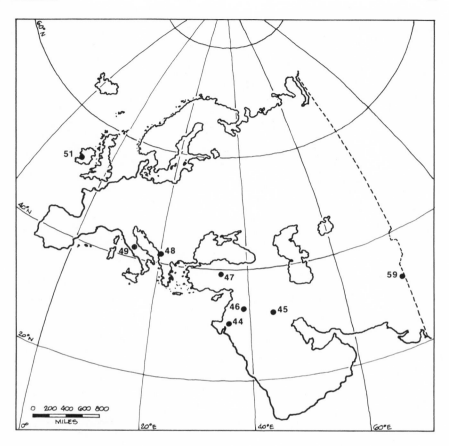

Figure 1.2. West Eurasia.

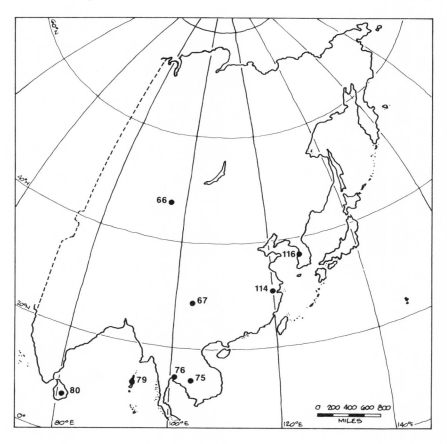

Figure 1.3. East Eurasia.

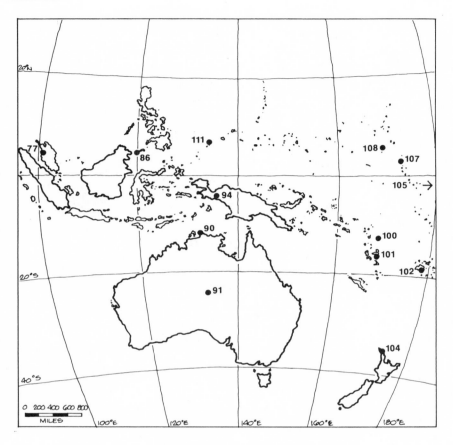

Figure 1.4 Insular Pacific.

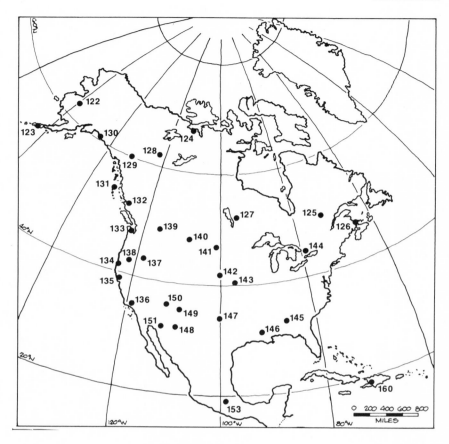

Figure 1.5. North America.

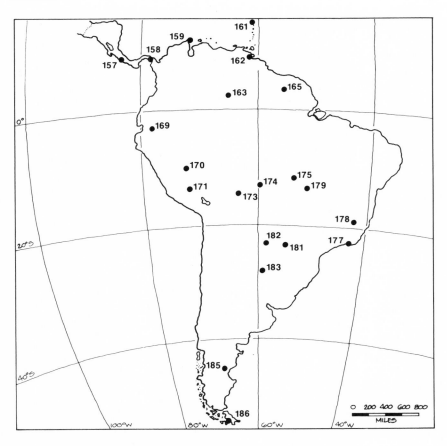

Figure 1.6. South America.

> If we consider polygyny to be a perquisite of leaders and a mark or measure of inequality, then in the world's so-called 'egalitarian' societies not all men are in fact equal. . . . That the relationship between people and control over strategic resources is central to understanding status differences in our own highly industrialized, materialist culture is insufficient reason to project these relationships back in evolutionary time and to suggest that all human status systems derive from struggles over the means and ends of production. Struggles in the Stone Age were . . . likely over the means and ends of reproduction.
>
> —Napoleon Chagnon (1979a:375)

2
INCIPIENT ASYMMETRIES

S ir Ronald Fisher, whose opinion began the last chapter, was both a natural scientist and a mathematician, and was struck by the difference in the kind of imagination evidenced by men and women in the two disciplines. Natural scientists, he thought, are confronted hands on from the first with an immense array of things; they begin with an empirical bias. Mathematicians, on the other hand, deal from the onset with abstractions, so that the thought of even the widest range of facts poses a limitation upon their ideas of the possible, and even, in the material sense, the impossible (1958:viii–ix). The history of anthropological theory would seem to belie that contradistinction. Anthropologists have not only conceived of a kind of human society yet to be discovered, they have continued to make variations on that conception central to their theorizations.

The group in which neither exclusive reproductive rights in wives nor productive rights in property exists (Morgan, 1877; Engels, 1884) has never turned up. Still, the idea that men in the simplest societies, unaffected by those since removed from the state of nature, enjoyed a form of "egalitarianism" persists. But, as Chagnon answered his own critical question: "Is reproductive success equal in egalitarian societies?'' (1979a)—clearly, it is not. Men accrue reproductive rights to wives of varying numbers and fertility in every human society. As Chagnon pointed out, the differential reproduction which follows must entail differences, not necessarily in *access* to strategic resources, but in *utilization* of them. A man with more dependent children must command more resources for his family's consumption. "That strategic resources are freely available to all, insofar as access to them is concerned, is simply beside the point. . . . The critical issue is consumption and utilization of resources, and not everybody is equal in these regards" (p. 378).

The critical questions remain: How are these inequalities determined? Do conflicts of interest exist in every human group? Do differences in strength, as the Darwinian hypothesis predicts, determine biases in their resolution? And do those biases, in turn, translate into reproduction? The evidence that follows addresses each of these questions. In answering them, the ethnographic record is convincingly redundant.

BIASED OUTCOMES

Conflicts of Interest

In the simplest societies, as in any society, conflicts of interest end in either avoidance or in direct confrontation. The former is, literally, actively pursued; but the latter is not infrequently resorted to. Richard Lee has recently written in detail about conflict and violence among the "harmless people" (Thomas, 1959) of the Kalahari. "Basically," Lee says, "the !Kung *are* a peace-loving people. . . . It is equally part of the story that the !Kung *do* fight and not infrequently with fatal results" (Lee, 1979:370). In three years, he recorded 58 case histories of arguments and fights; of them, 34 came to blows. Although homicide had stopped in the mid-1950s, probably largely as a result of outside intervention (p. 382), he was able to get recall information on 22 cases of homicide and 15 woundings occurring in the central !Kung interior between 1920 and 1955. He calculated that 22 killings over 50 years (*including* the 15 years since the killings had stopped!) in a base population of approximately 1500 yields a homicide rate of 29.3 per 100,000 person-years. This rate is high in comparison with other African figures; it is also high in relation to figures for the United States. Lee lists census bureau data showing a homicide rate in the United States of 9.2 per 100,000 population for 1972, and exceptionally high rates for Baltimore (36.8), Detroit (40.1), and Cleveland (41.3) (p. 398). As he points out, these figures would be much higher if wartime

fatalities were included in the calculations. However, as Turke and
Irons (in preparation) point out, if allowance is made for differences in
the population structures, the !Kung homicide rate would increase
relative to the rates in the United States. At any rate, the !Kung numbers
are high enough to make the point that they do not, or did not,
infrequently harm one another.

!Kung distinguish three standard levels of overt conflict: talking,
fighting, and deadly fighting. They also semantically distinguish forms
of increasingly aggressive "talk," the last of which is za, sexual insult-
ing; za is so climactic that it can lead directly to fighting or to group
fission or both. The second level of !Kung conflict involves wrestling
and punching, with the object of getting a headlock on an opponent and
forcing him to the ground. In these fights, men were almost three times
as likely to initiate the attack as women; and adultery was the most
common single cause. Finally, at the third level of conflict, fighting
with weapons, killers in all 22 recorded homicides were men between
the ages of 20 and 50. Fifteen of the killings were retaliatory; overwhelmingly, the precipitating cause of these feuds was women (p.383).
The !Kung motivation to look out for their Darwinian interests is, in this
respect, clearly in evidence.

The evidence suggests that conflicts of interest exist in all human
groups and when violence breaks out, these three levels are common
across cultures. In North Australia, Tiwi disputes often went no further
than the shouting of charges (Hart and Pilling, 1960:37); Brazilian
Trumai argued at one another across the evening men's circle, or,
standing in the village center, "hurled epithets and insults at each other
at the top of their voices" (Murphy and Quain, 1955:58). Similarly, in
eastern Polynesia, Marquesan opponents met before an audience, and,
standing apart, made "loud and long harangues, accompanied by the
most violent gesticulation" (Crook, n.d.:cxxxvii). Song duels are noto-
rious among Eskimos (see Hoebel, 1967); vituperative Tiv "drummed
the scandal" (Bohannan, 1957:142-144; 1967b); and South Pacific
Tikopians (Firth, 1939:269) composed and performed ridiculing songs
before as large an audience as was willing to listen.

Resolutions

When fights do break out, what determines the outcome? The answers are consistently three: kinship, wealth, and strength. Typically,
in southernmost South America, at Tierra del Fuego, any Yaghan who
found his relative or friend in a fight would come to his aid. Each man
sought his own justice, and found support among his circle of kin. "The
settlement of a dispute is determined more or less by club law. Every-

one is dependent upon himself and his nearest kinsfolk for his defense. . . . Decisions are, of course, not always just. . . . The law of the strongest prevails" (Gusinde, 1937:635). Although most fights took the form of an unarmed scuffle, 22 cases of homicide were recorded between 1871 and 1884. Though the sample is limited, the rate, which Cooper estimated at something like ten times as high as that of the United States (1946:95), is again sufficient to indicate that members of such a society had cause to fear occasional harm from one another. Again, according to Gusinde (1937:890), most murders were precipitated by a woman's adultery.

Similarly, Jenness found that, in a Copper Eskimo community, the maintenance of order "rests purely and simply on a basis of force. No man will commit a crime, save in the heat of passion, unless he believes that he can make good his escape until the affair blows over, or else that his kinsmen will support him against any attempt at revenge" (1922:96). In groups in which an individual's use of force on his own behalf is an option in resolving an argument, it becomes an obligation. Failure to retaliate against an offender was, to the Comanche, a social disgrace. "A man so acting was stamped not as magnanimous, but as lily-livered" (Hoebel, 1940:50). Coercion and force determined legality; and "ability to possess was nine points of the law" (p. 66).

Such an ability was evidenced in another widespread cross-cultural practice, called muru by the New Zealand Maori, and described in detail by Best. In brief, muru involved restitution by plunder. It was "an institution which provided for the exaction of compensation for offenses by the confiscation of property" (Firth, 1959:400). According to Best, "The mode of action was a wild rush of yelling, highly excited savages, who overran the premises and carried off anything portable that seemed desirable" (1924:359). Such a form of self-help, especially in the event of theft, apparently existed in a number of groups [e.g., see Nadel, 1947:151 (Otoro); Merker, 1910:281 (Masai); Spillius, 1959:6 (Tikopia); Whiting, 1950:78 (Paiute); Tooker, 1964:563 and Trigger, 1969:82 (Huron); and De Pineda, 1950:236-7 (Goajiro)].

Very generally, where there is no arbitrating authority, amassed strength determines the outcomes of conflicts, and strength is almost invariably determined by one's own physical prowess, and that represented by the aggregated force of one's kinship and alliance network. Among the most articulate expressions of that rule is that made in 1873 by California Klamath leader Henry Blow:

> Before the Bostons came there was no law. . . . It was a bad country in those times. Some men were bad and took away the property of other men. If a man was poor and had no friends, and had a beautiful squaw, some

stronger man would steal his squaw and kill him if he resisted. Might was right in those days and there was much fighting and killing everywhere. If a man was jealous because another was getting rich and had many friends, he would steal into his lodge and kill him when he was asleep, or lay in ambush to kill him as he went by. Those were bad times as we see now, since the Bostons have come and made law to protect every man's rights and property (quoted in Stern, 1965:21).

BIASED DECISIONS

Neither is self-interest sacrificed when arbiters arise. In cases in which an authority *is* capable of intervening, it is, again, almost always his own strength, wealth, and number of close kinsmen which effectively sanction his decisions. The association of property, family, and authority is repeated again and again in the ethnographies [some of many examples include Lee, 1979:344-346 (!Kung); Merker, 1910:287 (Masai); Ammar, 1954:60 (Haida); Lin, 1947:26 (Lolo); Radcliffe-Brown, 1922:45 (Andamanese); Linton, 1933:147-8 (Menabe); Spencer and Gillen, 1927:6 (Aranda); Firth, 1959:132 (Maori); La Barre, 1934:58 (Marquesans); Barnett, 1949:156 (Palauans); Pospisil, 1967 (Kapauku); Osgood, 1951:46 (Koreans); Birket-Smith and De Laguna, 1938:127 (Eyak); Spier, 1930:37 (Klamath); Opler, 1941:470 (Apache); De Pineda, 1950:168 (Goajiro); Chagnon, 1983, 1979a (Yanomamo)].

Cases

It follows that even in groups in which such an authority exists, he is often unable to enforce his decisions in opposition to the interests of a forceful faction. At the same time, where it affords sufficient sanction, he may be prone to bias decisions in favor of his own.

Among the Otoro of the Nuba hills in Africa, the intervention of the chief tended to supersede self-help. However, a thief, for example, might ignore the summons of a chief to give back stolen goods "if he thought himself strong enough to reject this interference" (Nadel, 1947:151). A chief then had to try to summon the support of a sufficient number of men to attack the thief and take back what had been stolen by force. According to Nadel, however, "a modified self-help continued to be practiced under Otoro chieftainship. The owner of the stolen property might still take the law into his own hands if he thought himself strong enough, and would only present a portion of his booty to the chief, thus buying his acquiescence" (p. 151).

Similarly, Pospisil relates a New Guinea Kapauku case in which a rich man charged a young boy 5 Km for a piglet, and then failed to deliver the pig. A stick fight ensued in which the authority fought against the wealthy man and his supporters; evidently, however, the rich man won, for the authority could not enforce his decision and the rich man went unpunished (1958:212).

Like the will of one individual, the will of several could be balked at by those backed by greater force. On the Moroccan Mediterranean coast, Riffians guilty of murder were obliged to allow the tribal council to burn down their houses and collect a $1000 fine. Occasionally, however, the murderer would resist, in which case the tribal council might have recourse to force. If a resistor, and his kinsmen, had no allies, they had not much of a chance; but there were few kin groups without friends. "The allies in the tribal council draw apart as inconspicuously and as quickly as possible and start shooting at the rest of the tribal council. The *bone* [kin group] which has refused sends messengers to talk with various councillors and to persuade them to join their side, promising money and women" (Coon, 1931:104-5). The result would be a confrontation between factions, which would end only when one side had won.

In many other cases in which an appeal to an arbiter is put forth, a powerful group might obtain a biased decision relative to another with relatively little amassed strength: compensations have been very generally awarded according to status. Among the East African Masai, "If in the district the fellow members of the lineage or tribe of the perpetrator have preponderance in numbers or power over those of the injured one, the fines are considerably smaller than in the opposite case," in which event murder, for example, would often be punished as negligent homicide, or even left unpunished (Merker, 1910:286). Among the Gheg of Albania, "The formula of 'one for one' was disregarded only in a few cases," i.e., when a man had killed his social superior, in which case his kin might take more than one life in turn (Hasluck, 1954:235). And among the Northwest Coast Twana, blood money varied again according to the victim's position. "A large and socially eminent kin group would be in a position to ask much more for the life of one of its members than would a smaller and socially weaker group of relatives" (Elmendorf, 1960:477).

Generally, decisions by an arbitrating authority on his own behalf have probably been sanctioned effectively by his own kinship network and wealth. Among, for instance, the Nama of southern Africa, attempted murder was punished by a hundred or more lashes, "unless the intended victim is the chief, when in former days the assailant was sentenced to death" (Schapera, 1930:344). Among the Alaskan Eyak, payment for homicide equaled a standard amount, regardless of the victim's age or sex, "since all human life was recorded of equal value." On the other hand, "For the murder of a chief (or a member of his family?), however, a greater payment was required" (Birket-Smith and De Laguna, 1938:142). Finally, Maybury-Lewis conveys a dramatic case in which his faction enforced a self-interested decision by a Shavante chief. According to Maybury-Lewis, Shavante chieftaincy was consti- tuted of no more than a practical recognition of where the power lay: a chief whose faction lost the power to maintain him in his position forfeited his right to his office. Groups could take action against an individual only if his faction disowned him, or found itself powerless to do otherwise than to give in to his punishment. "Once a man is either disowned or abandoned by his faction, then *he is virtually outlawed*" (1967:189; emphasis added). In order to avenge against a supposed death by sorcery, a Shavante chief, Apewe, directed his supporters to kill those he held responsible. These included eight men, who were slaughtered in a single night. "This massacre horrified even the Shavante" (p. 187). According to Maybury-Lewis, Apewe used his brother's death as a pretext for annihilating an opposing faction.

The evidence, then, is clear on two points. First, where the strength of an authority is less than that of an opponent, the opponent wins a confrontation; and second, where the strength of an authority is greater than his opponent's, the authority will bias the resolution of disputes in the interests of the more powerful group. One of the most powerful of these probably most often represents his own, his kinsmen's, and his allies' interests.

Causes

KINSHIP, WEALTH, AND STRENGTH.   The Darwinian significance of aid from kin in settling a score is clear, given that kinship has a genetic component. But the use of classificatory kinship terminology to order social relations in many societies calls this conclusion into question (e.g., Sahlins, 1976b). Theoretically, the "brother" who offers assistance could be a distant parallel cousin, as well as a full sib. Addressing this problem, Chagnon and Bugos (1979) analyzed a filmed Yanomamo ax fight (Asch and Chagnon, 1975), which took place among the members of two visiting villages in Venezuela. They found that genealogical kinship [a variation on Sewall Wright's (1922) inbreeding coefficient] was a significant predictor of willingness to come to either principal's aid. Besides offering aid in a confrontation, genealogical kin are prob- ably most willing to share labor (e.g., Hames, 1979, 1982; Essock-Vitale and McGuire, 1980, 1985; Berté, 1983) and resources (e.g., Silk, 1980; Betzig and Turke, 1985a). In a group in which there is no accumulable wealth, the number and types of kin available to help provide labor may often be the best predictor of ability to garner resources (Chagnon, 1979a; Berté, 1983), and to obtain mates (Chagnon, 1982). That "fraternal interest groups" use kinship as a basis of organization, to defend common interests, has already been stressed in much anthroplogical work (see van Velzen and van Wetering, 1960; discussion and references in Paige and Paige, 1981:53-67).

The consistent importance of friendship and wealth in alliance formation can also easily be understood in Darwinian terms. Wealth may be seen as a reservoir of potential reciprocity, friendship as just another word for it. Ability to "buy" support from allies is not infrequently mentioned in ethnographic accounts of the aggressive resolution of conflicts. "Wealth," in such cases, may best be valued in terms of its likely effects on an individual's reproduction; the ability to exchange daughters as wives, for example, may be understood to be one important source of wealth. In the Riffian case, Coon explicitly notes that fractious factions promised potential backers money and, significantly, wives.

Finally, the conflict of interest which calls strength and allegiance to task is as common cross culturally as they are in biasing outcomes. In the words of Confucius, "Disorder does not come from heaven, but is brought about by women." A statement to that effect may exist in most ethnographic accounts. Notoriously, the major precipitating cause of club fights among the Yanomamo is: conflict over women (e.g., Chagnon, 1983:119). Disputes over women "stand apart" among modern Turks, invariably calling for violence (Stirling, 1965:270); elopements may lead to physical fighting among the Mohla in the Western Punjab (Eglar, 1960:18); adultery is regarded as the most serious crime among the Semang (Schebesta, 1928:280); and over 90% of Tiwi disputes were matters in which women were somehow involved (Hart and Pilling, 1960:90). Among Kapauku, Pospisil noted that most *wars* start because of violations of a husband's exclusive sexual rights (1958:167); Linton found Marquesan killings followed two motives: sexual jealousy and revenge (1939:176). Among the Saramacca of the upper Suriname River basin, quarrels over women were more frequent than any other kinds of disputes (Kahn, 1931:97); and among Trumai, "the chief source of conflict in the village was sex" (Murphy and Quain, 1955:58).

Contrary, again, to prior expectation (Morgan, 1877: Engels, 1884), communal rights in reproduction have yet to be evidenced. True to the Darwinian prediction, the evidence suggests that in virtually all societies, women are a significant cause of male conflicts of interest. Darwin himself anticipated this conclusion. "With savages . . . the women are the constant cause of war both between members of the same tribe and between distinct tribes" (1871:871). In defending his right to a woman, to his property, or to his life, a man must consistently rely on kinship, wealth, and strength.

SEX AND AGE. Two other widely acknowledged determinants of conflict resolution have been sex and age. Engels, for example, argued that the first class opposition in history coincided with the development of the antagonism between men and women, and that "the first class oppression coincides with that of the female sex by the male" (1884 [1964]:58; cf. Morgan, 1877 [1978]:79; Marx and Engels, 1845 [1976]:33). More recent proponents of the idea that simple society is "egalitarian" (e.g., Fried, 1967; Terray, 1972) emphasize, too, that status differentiation in such societies springs from differences in age and sex. Elder male authority is extended from the family to the extended family to the society at large. This fact also is consistent with Darwinian arguments.

Males may be expected to forcefully prevent fertile females from soliciting or giving in to advances by competing males. And male–male competition for the greater physiological share of reproductive invest- ment by females may be expected to increase as ecological and social conditions enable successful males to be polygynous (Emlen and Oring, 1977; cf. Verner and Willson, 1966; Orians, 1969). Consistently, evi- dence from a number of primate societies indicates that male domi- nance is largely a function of polygyny or promiscuity, and, in seasonal breeders, may be manifested during the breeding season only (Hrdy, 1981, chapter 4; cf. Darwin, 1871:575, 915). In truly monogamous species (a classification from which *Homo sapiens* historically has been exempt), male dominance is less likely to be a fact of life (Hrdy, 1981).

Where males follow mating with parenting, they have an especially high reproductive stake in ensuring a biological relationship to their progeny; this is, again, characteristic of the human species (see Trivers, 1972; Alexander, 1974, 1977, 1979; Greene, 1978; Kurland, 1979). Accordingly, cross culturally, men often exercise their additional height, weight, and strength to intimidate spouses against infidelity, and to punish them, often severely, for transgressions. Broude and Greene (1976) have shown that in standard sample societies a consis- tent male-biased double-standard in extramarital sex exists. Women may be least likely to tolerate such asymmetry where they have the least to gain from consorts in the form of support, including heritable support, for themselves and their descendants, and where they have the greatest number of supportive kin. Where men have the most to offer, in terms of reproductive investment, they may be in a position to demand the most from a woman: they may, for example, insist on patrilocal residence, away from her kinsmen (Richards, 1950; Driver, 1956; Gaulin and Schlegel, 1980; Flinn, 1981) and on patrilineal inher- itance (see Bachofen, 1861; Morgan, 1871; Engels, 1884; Tylor, 1889; Murdock, 1949; Aberle, 1961; Hartung, 1976, 1982; Gaulin and

Schlegel, 1980; Flinn, 1981), and punish her most severely for adultery, maximally, ensuring her fidelity by keeping her cloistered (Dickemann, 1981) and enforcing her monogamy (e.g., Bachofen, 1861; Morgan, 1871; Engels, 1884). Gaulin and Schlegel (1980) and Flinn (1981) have shown statistically that where women and their children receive substantial proportions of support from kinsmen as opposed to husbands, they also engage more freely in adultery; they may as well be more willing to divorce (e.g., Gluckman, 1950; Flinn, 1981).

Competition among men over women results in sexual selection: men most successful should spread the traits which enabled them to outreproduce their competitors (Darwin, 1871; Campbell, 1972, especially Trivers, 1972). For males of most species, size is a factor affecting the outcome of such competition. Alexander, Hoogland, Howard, Noonan, and Sherman (1979) have compiled evidence suggesting that in pinnipeds, ungulates, primates in general, and the human primate in particular, the extent to which male body length exceeds that of females is directly related to the size of the harem of a successful male. Humans, again, may generally be considered somewhat polygynous; cross culturally, men tend to be taller than women by about 5 to 12% (p. 415). This size dimorphism may bias the resolution of conflicts of interest with a woman in favor of a man; so might a number of sex differences in physiology and psychology, which have sometimes been argued to be products of sexual selection (see, e.g., Maccoby and Jacklin, 1974; Symons, 1979; Gaulin and Fitzgerald, 1985). None of these sex differences in themselves, of course, constitutes a motive for competition.

Like sex, age initially confers difference in size; in a social species, it may also confer advantages in knowledge and material accumulation. All of these differences, as Alexander (1974) has pointed out, amount to a phenotypic advantage of parents over their children. Elder males may predictably be able to bias the resolution of conflicts in their own interest.

Although, in this sample, a systematic bias by age in the resolution of conflicts has been detailed in only one case, it is a classic: the male gerontocracy held a virtual monopoly of power among the North Australian Tiwi. The most frequent disputes were between young and old men, in which the latter accused the former of seduction. In such events, a "one-sided duel" was staged. Encircled by an audience of 60 or 70 spectators, the accuser, an old man, covered in white paint and holding hunting and ceremonial spears, faced the defendant, a young man, in little or no paint, "perhaps holding a spear or two in his hand (a sign of insolence), perhaps holding only throwing sticks (less defiant . . .), or perhaps entirely weaponless (a sign of proper humility and deference to his seniors that all bachelors ought to show in such situations)" (Hart and Pilling, 1960:81). The old man would let loose his spears; following varying degrees of resistance the young man *must* allow himself to be hit. Should the defendant's resistance be too great, senior men would gradually leave the spectator ranks and line up with the accuser, spears in hand, while the full brothers or father of the young man would also come forward from the audience, stand beside him and attempt to restrain him from harm.

Even here, though, kinship too was taken into consideration. Generally, the younger man, being a bachelor, would be without affinal ties or dependents; the older man would be in possession of both. Nevertheless, in making an accusation against his adversary, an elder man had to weigh more than his seniority. "Like a good lawyer in our own culture, the old man had to consider, before he took the matter to court, who the young man was and who his friends and relatives were, and had to ask himself whether in seeking vengeance for the blow to his pride [sic] he might not be doing himself more political harm than the injury was worth" (p. 38).

Increasing Asymmetries

Advantages in kinship and wealth go up with hierarchical complexity. These in turn afford ability to bias the outcomes of conflicts of interest to an increasing extent. Sir Henry Maine long ago supposed that ancient "law" was not a product of social contract, "a theory which, though nursed into importance by political passions, derived all its sap from the speculations of lawyers" (1864:299). Rather, he thought, rights and obligations have always coincided with relative status.

As imbalances in power grow, inequities do in fact become increasingly striking. Among other techniques, chiefs may have come to make good use of supernatural sanction, including accusations of witchcraft, to eliminate undesirable others. Trigger (1969) made the egalitarian nature of the Huron confederacy, given its size, which in 1610 embraced 20,000, a theme of his ethnography. Nevertheless, tribe members had to be willing to respect the right of chiefs and the tribal council to kill "antisocial" members of the tribe without response. "Chiefs are reported threatening individuals whose behavior had elicited their disapproval (mainly the Jesuits and their converts) that they would accuse them of witchcraft and see they were killed unless they changed their ways. . . . Sometimes it appears that when a person was judged guilty, the verdict was pronounced *in absentia* and an executioner was appointed to kill him without warning" (p. 88). Similarly, a California Yokut chief "always had money. . . . If he got short of money, he would have his doctor kill somebody who was rich. . . . We usually had good chiefs with good doctors, but sometimes even a good chief

would bribe a doctor to kill some man he thought ought to be killed"
(Gayton, 1948:95).

Often, though, men in power effected inequity without any recourse
to higher authority. In northern South America, when a Goajiro husband and his rival died in the struggle over a woman, the richer and
more important family demanded compensation payment, even if they
were the lover's kin. Should a husband survive and the lover perish, the
husband paid for the death, "especially if the dead man's relatives
belonged to a group of superior status" (De Pineda, 1950:236). If they
could not pay, the dead man's kin, without negotiation, could raze and
destroy their property, and steal "everything it could lay its hands on."
Such unfairness could be carried to a ludicrous extent, as in the
following case:

> A rich Indian living in Nazaret got drunk one day. Already very intoxi-
> cated, he started off for home at nightfall, riding on a very frisky burro. For
> some reason the animal got frightened on the road, near a fence of sticks
> which protected a corn field belonging to a family different from his own.
> Because of the jumping of his mount and his own condition, the Indian fell
> off and scratched his face on the fence, and received in addition several
> wounds caused by the out-of-control animal. The injured Goajiro charged
> the owners of the fence with the responsibility of his having shed blood
> and to indemnify him for this involuntary spilling of his blood, the owners
> of the sown field were punished by the destruction of their fence, which
> meant that they lost their harvest. The owners, of a group inferior to that of
> the injured man, had to resign themselves to this punishment for fear of
> worse sanctions (De Pineda, 1950:218-219).

Among the New Zealand Maori, formerly, chiefs of distinction
would occasionally call upon others to offer them labor or resources of
their own. "This was a gift from free men, not tribute from vassals, and
was probably made in recognition of the leading position of the chief in
his tribe" (Firth, 1959:296). In one instance, a chief sent messengers out
in quest of preserved birds for his use. People came with calabashes for
his inspection, one of which was only a little more than half full. " 'Now
a full case was the proper thing to present. To offer less was to
whakahawea or despise the recipient.' As a result the man whose
calabash was lacking in quantity was afterwards slain by order of Te
Akitu [the chief] and thus supplemented in his own person the inadequate gift of supplies. No attempt was made to avenge his death"
(ibid).

Finally, in Tikopia bias in the outcomes of conflicts of interest was
firmly entrenched. Firth sums it up: "Tikopia is an example of a
community which has had a differential application of sanctions. Not
only has the principle of ignoring the trivial (de minimum non carat

lex) been in vogue. Another principle, which might be phrased as *de maximum non licet lex*, the non-validity of the law as it concerns the greatest personages, has also been applied" (1959:337). The general principle in Tikopia operative in 1929 and in 1952 was that members of chiefly lineages could commit acts of violence, especially against commoners, with little or no likelihood of vengeance, while a commoner who committed an act of aggression against a person of chiefly lineage was liable for major punishment (p. 307). For major offenses, Tikopians were compelled to commit suicide by canoeing or, in a woman's case, swimming out to sea. The chief offense for which men were so compelled was that of being discovered in an intrigue with the daughter of a chief (Rivers, 1914:306). Other offenses meriting this penalty included striking a chief's son in a quarrel, and disregarding his welfare in a crisis (Firth, 1949:179). Lesser offenses against authority included those falling under the rubric of disturbing the chief's peace. These embraced a range of "anti-social" actions, among them making a loud noise where a chief was sitting or sleeping, going to sea in a canoe without his permission, failing to carry out any of a chief's orders, or failing to show proper respect. In a meeting, or *fono*,

> Every head should be bowed when the Ariki Tafua appears. But occasionally the rule is broken. If a chief catches sight of an upturned face as he strides on to the marae he calls out to the offender "Who is the person who looks on the *fono* of the gods?" The culprit, it is said, is overcome at the disgrace of discovery. "Very great is the shame of the man." Immediately he rises from his seat and hurries away to the beach. There he hauls down his canoe, and paddles out to sea to commit suicide. . . . [But this,] in fact, was the theoretical rather than the actual outcome. Going to his gardens and orchards, the offender strips them of large quantities of taro, breadfruit, bananas, and coconuts, and prepares several great baskets of fruit. Assisted by his relatives he bears these at the end of the day to the Ariki Tafua. Then, wailing his humility, he crawls to the chief over the floor mats, presses his nose to the chief's feet and knee and follows this by the chanting of a dirge. Thus he abases himself and by the presentation of the food is absolved from any further consequences of his fault (Firth, 1940:203).

PERKS FOR THE ARBITERS

As such asymmetries grow, arbiters are more and more likely to accrue the additional benefits of perquisites in fines, fees, bribes, and confiscations, for the trouble of resolving conflicts, generally in their own interests. At first, in less hierarchical groups, this compensation is not great, and may be seen as a relatively fair return on services rendered. As power differences augment the arrangement is, however, increasingly subject to exploitation.

Typically, fines levied in criminal cases go to chiefs, or are shared between a chief and his judges, as in the Nama case (Schapera, 1930:334). Northern Nigerian Tiv often paid "day-fines," usually a goat, to authorities upon judgment. The meat was divided among the chief and elders, after which they went home. "In the old days, the elders and their chief were of one mind" (East, 1939:346). An Otoro chief not only received a part of the booty when a man helped himself to a thief's property, but shared in the division of such property when he himself had raised the force necessary to restore to their owner stolen goods (Nadel, 1947:151). And among the Albanian Gheg, half the value of a stolen article was divided among the elders who tried the case (Durham, 1928:71). Chiefs or elders are explicitly said to have been entitled to collect fines in connection with various offenses among the Masai of East Africa (Maguire, 1928:12-13), Konso of Ethiopia (Hallpike, 1972:137), Ahaggaren Tuareg of northern Africa (Nicolaisen, 1959:110-111), Moroccan Riffians (Coon, 1931:104), Rwala of Syria and Jordan (Musil, 1928:437), Menabe Tanala of Madagascar (Linton, 1933:149), Great Lakes Huron (Trigger, 1969:86), and Haida of the northern Northwest Coast (Niblack, 1888:253).

A Goajiro thief was punished by taking away his livestock, which, leaving him without a livelihood, forced him to emigrate. Adding insult to retribution, his abandoned lands were then confiscated by his enemies (De Pineda, 1950:240). In addition to the products of orchards deferred to them by offenders against their "peace," and therefore against society, Tikopian chiefs received mats, cord, fish hooks, and wooden bowls (Firth, 1959:307). And, on Makin and Butiritari Islands in the Gilberts, it was said that the chief had no lands, only the use of such could be assessed as fines (Stevenson, 1901:68). According to Lambert (1966:166), the Butiritari chief on rare occasions would exercise his right to confiscate land as a fine. The right of an authority to perquisites in connection with the settling of disputes is, of course, only part of the privilege he might accrue in his office (e.g., Betzig, 1985).

PERKS FOR THE WINNERS

As Chagnon pointed out, unequal access to the basic resource which *perpetuates* life, members of the opposite sex, is a condition in the simplest societies (1979a). If men in all societies compete for the means to reproduction, *do* the most successful enjoy rights to a disproportionate share of women? They certainly do.

Shinbone, the renowned Venezuelan Yanomamo pater, exemplifies the high end of reproductive variation toward which males in simple societies may aspire. Shinbone, according to Chagnon's extensive genealogies, had 43 children. In the course of his research, Chagnon discovered why members of the Bisaasi-teri village in which he lived thought of the entire Shamatari population as his descendants: "A very large fraction of them were" (p. 379). Shinbone's father had 14 children, 143 grandchildren, 335 great grandchildren, and, at the time of Chagnon's last census in 1975, 401 great great grandchildren. As a result of being a member of a large kin group and the descendant of an influential man, a scion of such as Shinbone may have had a reproductive edge as well. Chagnon found that men with large numbers of ascending and own generation kin were most likely to be polygynous themselves (1982). Again, should a conflict of interest over women come to blows, the advantage may go to the man with the greater number of close kin (Chagnon and Bugos, 1979). Headmen are predictably polygynous men (Chagnon, 1980).

Similarly, Maybury-Lewis found that the Brazilian Shavante chief, Apewe, having been married to at least five different women, although to no more than three simultaneously, had had an exceptionally large number of children. His offspring constituted a remarkably high proportion of the total population of his village (Maybury-Lewis, 1967; see too Salzano, Neel, and Maybury-Lewis, 1967). Maybury-Lewis notes, "There is no doubt that Shavante men like to have more than one wife" (p. 77). If a man has enough good fortune and prestige he may continue to take a series of wives throughout his life. Should they bear him sons, they increase his potential prestige by making him the head of a strong lineage, which in turn might make it possible to take additional wives.

Statements to the effect that men take as many wives as they can defend and support are repeated throughout ethnographic accounts. In hunting and gathering groups, this may be determined largely by ability to provide meat. Among the !Kung, "The number of wives a man may have is not regulated by social rules but by his ability to obtain and support them," especially as evidenced by hunting success (Marshall, 1959:346). Classically, among Copper Eskimos, "Very few men have more than one wife each. Polygyny increases their responsibilities and the labour required of them; moreover, it subjects them to a great deal of jealousy and ill-feeling, especially on the part of men who cannot find wives for themselves. The Eskimo polygamist, therefore, must be a man of great energy and skill in hunting, bold and unscrupulous, always ready to assert himself and uphold his position by an appeal to force" (Jenness, 1922:161). These have been undoubtedly ecumenical prerequisites for polygynous males.

As men accumulate property, wealth too largely determines their ability to live polygynously. As Pospisil points out, among the Kapauku, wealthy men tend to have larger families because of polygyny, and also because their children are better nourished and so have a better chance to survive (1963:303). It is probably reasonable to suspect that family survivability has been another general perquisite of leadership.

As a rule, the evidence is overwhelming that rich and powerful men do enjoy the greatest degree of polygyny cross culturally [e.g., Schapera, 1930:251 (Nama); Nadel, 1947:116 (Otoro); Hollis, 1905:303 (Masai); Hallpike, 1972:105 (Konso); Coon, 1931:142 (Riffians); Lin, 1947:62 (Lolo); Linton, 1933:132 (Menabe); Firth, 1936:132 (Tikopia); Lane and Lane, n.d.:9 (Bunlap); Best, 1924:448 (Maori); Barnett, 1979:60 (Palauans); Osgood, 1958:200 (Ingalik); Veniaminov, 1840:60 (Aleut); Turner, 1894:270 (Montagnais); Denys, 1908:410-411 (Micmac); Hallowell, 1955:300 (Saulteaux); Honigmann, 1954:132 (Kaska); Niblack, 1888:367 (Haida); McIlwraith, 1948:144 (Bellacoola); Elmendorf, 1960:367 (Twana); Heizer and Mills, 1932:128 (Yurok); Loeb, 1926:243 (Pomo); Gayton, 1948:94 (Yokuts); Whiting, 1950:100 (Paiute); Spier, 1930:49 (Klamath); Bowers, 1965:155 (Hidatsa); Fletcher and La Flesche, 1906:326 (Omaha); Opler, 1941:416 (Chiricahua Apache); James, 1903:229 (Havasupai); Stout, 1947:27 (Cuna); Wilbert, 1958:60 (Goajiro); Du Tertre, 1667:16 (Callinago); Turrado Moreno, 1945:254 (Warrau); Herskovits and Herskovits, 1934:159 (Saramacca); Holmberg, 1950:58-59 (Siriono); Levi-Strauss, 1948:67 (Nambicuara); Watson, 1952:117 (Cayua); Musters, 1873:187 (Tehuelche)]. "Polygamy . . . is almost universally followed by the leading men in every tribe" (Darwin, 1871:896). Irons (1979a), Flinn (1983), Wrangham and Ross (1983), Essock-Vitale (1984), and Turke and Betzig (1985), have recently demonstrated relationships among wealth, multiple mates, and reproductive success quantitatively.

Besides the advantages of polygyny and possibly higher offspring survivability, powerful men may enjoy an additional reproductive asymmetry. They may have privileged access to more fertile, more attractive, wives (e.g., Borgerhoff Mulder, 1985). That these should be synonymous is no surprise; it is reasonable to suppose that men attracted to nubile women historically left more descendants than those with alternate tastes (Williams, 1975; Symons, 1979:192).

Again, the Tiwi are the classic case; old men retained a virtual monopoly over nubile women. Rather like Hamadryas baboons (Kummer, 1968), they took them on as children. As a result, they not infrequently widowed them. Older, widowed women were the only wives of which a young Tiwi man was generally able to avail himself. Until he was in his late thirties, it was unlikely that any father-in-law would consider him worthy of being bequeathed a younger daughter (Hart and Pilling, 1960). This asymmetry is mirrored in other societies.

Among Nambicuara of Mato Grosso, the regular removal of young women by chiefs from the marriage cycle created a "permanent unbalance" between the number of young men and women of marriageable age. "Young men are the chief victims of that situation and must either remain bachelors for several years or marry widows or old women discarded by their husbands" (Levi-Strauss, 1944:27). And again, on the northern North American plains, all Gros Ventre girls were married before puberty, usually as wives to older men with independent households (Flannery, 1953:172). Young men just starting their careers have been encouraged to look among the older women for wives [cf., e.g., Lane and Lane, n.d.:12 (Bunlap); Cushing, 1882:551 (Havasupai); Eglar, 1960:92 (Punjabi)].

For men at the opposite end of social privilege from those having what it takes to marry many, young women, fraternal polyandry may have been resorted to as an option (see Alexander, 1974; Van den Berghe, 1979). Although the compromise it represents is severe, a share in a reproductive resource may be better than none at all. Where it does occur, polyandry is probably most often among brothers. This, of course, is consistent with the Darwinian theory of nepotism; investment in a niece or nephew is better in the reproductive sense than investment in a nonrelative. Ethnographic examples indicate that only in return for rendering essential economic assistance to the household would a brother be given reproductive rights in a wife. For instance, in northwestern Canada, Kaska polyandry apparently was restricted to old men unable to hunt sufficiently to support their families. "As the informant expressed it, 'Sometimes a man cannot feed all the children of his wife. He then asks a brother to stay with him and trap with him and help him feed his family'" (Honigmann, 1954:133). Even then, brothers were not supposed to have had sexual relations with the woman unless her first husband was absent. Interestingly, in this case, the children of a polyandrous household were supposed to belong to the genetic father. Nevertheless, the assignment could never be certain, and relationships were said to be susceptible to jealousy. Contrary to the impressions of many, who have traditionally focused on variations in behavior between, rather than within, societies (see Murdock, 1972), polyandry, especially fraternal polyandry, has probably been an option for less well-endowed men in a number of groups [e.g., Veniaminov, 1840:78 (Aleut); Park, 1937:366 (Paiute); Dorsey and Murie, 1940:85 (Pawnee)].

In exceptional cases, reproductive access to a wife may have been given up solely in exchange for needed wealth or labor, without the compensating factor of relatedness between the co-husbands. One such exception may have been the Marquesan system (but see Handy, 1923).

Wealthy households have been said to have included eleven to twelve men and only three or four women; secondary husbands in this instance have been suggested to have functioned as little more than servants. According to Thompson [1841 (1980):26], few landless lower classmen ever had their own wives or women; instead, "they commonly live promiscuously, or attach themselves as a friend (for they spurn the name servant) to some householder, do the menial work of the house, and then his master's wife becomes the joint wife of both." According to La Barre, second "husbands" had sexual access to a chief's wife only when chiefs were absent (1934:53); even in this instance, they may have functioned as "guardians of her virtue," in return for which they themselves had limited sexual access to her (cf. Hughes, 1982). That polyandry existed at all in the Marquesan case has been seriously questioned (e.g., Handy, 1923). That, if it did, Marquesan men with the means to reproduce did not compromise their reproductive interests by risking cuckoldry to a greater extent than men without is indicated by the assertion that adultery was punished only in the royal family by death (La Barre, 1934:59).

Most broadly, this form of bias, a differential tolerance of a wife's infidelity according to a husband's ability to provide, is frequently alluded to in the ethnographies (see Dickemann, 1981). On the upper Missouri, no Hidatsa village leader would consider risking his "reputation" by marrying a woman who had carried on numerous affairs with other men. He therefore chose a young girl strictly trained by her parents. "He would keep close watch of her and usually enlisted his clansmen and society to do likewise" (Bowers, 1965:155). To this end she would accompany him on hunting trips, visits to nearby camps, and even on war expeditions. Another mirror-image example comes from Levi-Strauss, who found that secondary wives of chiefs among the Nambicuara did not follow the standard sexual division of work pattern, under which the first wife labored. Generally, secondary wives, who belonged to a younger generation, and who were chosen by the chief from among the prettiest and healthiest girls of the group, "disdain domestic tasks and remain idle, either playing with the children to whose generation they belong or flirting with their husband, while the first wife keeps busy with the food and the fire." When the chief left on an exploration, such as a hunt, they would go with him, bringing him "their moral and physical help" (1944:27).

Finally, Kapauku husbands formerly were supposed to have killed their unfaithful spouses without exception. Women, however, have been unexceptionally expensive in Kapauku society; recently, only the wealthiest men could afford to continue this custom [Pospisil,

1958:285; cf. Hollis, 1905:312 (Masai); Stevenson, 1901:248-53 (Gilberts)].

Conversely, it might be safe to assume that wealthy and powerful men were in a position to commit adultery themselves with differential impunity [see Murphy and Quain, 1955 (Trumai)]. Evidence from more hierarchical societies suggests that, at least eventually, this may have become a general phenomenon.

Men with strong social advantages may have enjoyed another reproductive edge. They may have exercised the right to commit "incest," or to break prescriptive or preferential marriage rules (Needham, 1962), thereby making available a larger pool of potential wives. The neatest example of this comes again from the Kapauku. Pospisil narrates the following case:

> The protagonist of our story is Awiitigaaj, the headman of the village of Botukebo, a prosperous pig breeder, a courageous war leader, and an enthusiast about feminine beauty. Like any connoisseur, he collected some extremely valuable specimens by marrying ten of the most attractive women in the Kamu Valley. Unfortunately, he discovered the incest taboo—which prohibits marrying an individual of the same sib—would deprive his collection of at least one outstanding example of female pulchritude. Nevertheless, in 1935, he did not hesitate to break the taboo. . . . The seducer's relatives were absolved from payment of the bride price by being forced to fight. This release from their obligations induced them to accept and recognize the incestuous union (1958:832-833).

Following his own precedent, the protagonist later contracted two more incestuous unions. Saffirio, Chagnon, and Betzig (1982) have similarly shown that by manipulating village fissioning patterns and kinship terms, elder Yanomamo men most successfully increase the number of their "cross," as opposed to "parallel" kinsmen and kinswomen, and so their reservoir of available wives (see also Chagnon, 1972, 1982, 1983). And Fredlund (1985) has demonstrated that whether or not Yanomamo marriages were contracted according to preference, they were least likely to be called "incestuous" by closely related kinsmen.

One more possibility of reproductive bias in societies in which status differences are well established: well to do parents might have had more descendants by investing preferentially in sons over daughters, and low-status parents by favoring daughters over sons. The logic is Trivers and Willard's (1973; cf. Alexander, 1974; Dickemann, 1979a). Again, because of the different physiological stake in investment between the sexes, successful men can parent many more children than successful women. On the other hand, it follows that, given a roughly even sex ratio (see Fisher, 1958), an unsuccessful man will have fewer children than an unsuccessful woman. Well to do parents, then, being able to transfer their resources to reproductively successful children, may produce more grandchildren by favoring sons; and low-status parents may do the same by biasing their investment toward daughters.

In a brilliant paper, Mildred Dickemann (1979a) has shown that in some highly stratified groups, this prediction is dramatically borne out. By practicing female-biased infanticide, upper strata parents produce more sons, and are able to bequeath them the lion's share of their abundant resources. Even in much smaller, nonstratified societies, new evidence suggests that this prediction may hold. Chiefs, wealthy men, and their wives might associate preferentially with their sons, and less materially privileged parents more with their daughters (Betzig and Turke, 1985b).

The exploitation of personal strength in such societies has disturbed a number of observers. They have asked for a "common power to keep us all in awe," (Hobbes, 1651) to lay down the law. Heads of many leveled hierarchies were bequeathed that authority; their actions were not always in the interests of the majority.

> So Samuel told all the words of the Lord to the people who were asking a king from him. He said, "These will be the ways of the king who will reign over you: he will take your sons and appoint them to his chariots and to be his horsemen, and to run before his chariots; and he will appoint for himself commanders of thousands and commanders of fifties, and some to plow his ground and to reap his harvest, and to make his implements of war and the equipment of his chariots. He will take your daughters to be perfumers and cooks and bakers. He will take the best of your fields and vineyards and olive orchards and give them to his servants. He will take your menservants and maidservants, and the best of your cattle and your asses, and put them to his work. He will take the tenth of your flocks, and you shall be his slaves. And in that day you will cry out because of your king, whom you have chosen for yourselves; but the Lord will not answer you in that day."
>
> —1 Samuel 8:10-18

3

DESPOTISM

The facts about kings, the extent of their privilege, the numbers of their wives, and the use of their power to kill commoners without cause or consequence, are subject to only a narrow range of argument. The right emphasis on and interpretation of those facts, on the other hand, are liable to wide deliberation. In every case, there is the potential for a rationale in the form of a Plinian panegyric, and for a Juvenalian satyrization. In many cases, including the Roman, both have been done. The former often is written in retrospect, or by a patrician; the latter comes from contemporaneous accounts, or from the much greater, though less prolific, masses of plebeians.

In his study of Dahomey, Herskovits stressed this difference in perspective. He found in accounts of the regimes of kings what he considered two extremes of overstatement. One view, which he termed the Abomey attitude, was held by members of the royal sib or descendants of men who held high office under the kings. It was "replete with

tales of splendor, of wisdom, and of daring." The alternate view, of
those from more provincial regions, recounted "oppression, cruelty,
and the insecurity felt by those not in power" (1938:22). Authorities
over these territories are said to have wielded despotic power in their
own jurisdictions (p. 29), and to have taken perquisites from their
subjects in connection with arbitration. Of the head of provincial
Whydah, Herskovits says, "He is great at embezzlement, and woe betide
the litigious wight whose case falls into his hands" (p. 28). Consistently, contemporary accounts of central authority in Abomey all
stressed the absolutism of a king's rule once he found himself securely
on the throne (p. 32). "As with any despot," any infraction against his
whim, however unreasonsable, was severely punished (p. 36).

Evidently, such punishments were not altogether infrequent. Duncan, in 1847, recounted his arrival in Abomey. Near the marketplace, he
saw a corpse impaled on a post in an upright position; further on he saw
two more, in a state of decomposition, hung by their feet. "The vulture
was industriously endeavouring to satisfy his appetite, but the heat of
the sun had dried the skin so as to render it impenetrable to his efforts"
(p. 219). On the opposite side of the market he found another pair of
corpses similarly displayed, with the exception that they had also been
subject to mutilation. Duncan was "surprised" at these exhibitions as in
Abomey decapitation, after which bodies were dragged away from town
and thrown into a pit to be disposed of more immediately by vultures
and wolves (p. 252), was the favored method of execution (p. 220). On
inquiry, he found that the men in the marketplace had been found
guilty of adultery with one of the king's wives.

As societies have grown hierarchically, men and women have come
into sufficient power to inflict substantial fines and even penalties of
death upon culpable subjects. They have also been increasingly capable
of behaving despotically, of robbing and injuring their subjects completely arbitrarily. How often was that power abused? In this chapter,
that question is asked of each of the most hierarchical preindustrial
societies in the sample.

DESPOTIC SOCIETIES

Babylonians

The primary source on Babylonian government of the second mil-
lennium B.C. is both aristocratic and abstract: despotism is not in
evidence in the Code of Hammurabi. Rather, "That the strong may not
oppress the weak (and) so to give justice to the orphan (and) the widow,
I have inscribed my precious words . . . , to judge the judgement of the

land (and) decide the decision of the land (and) so to give justice to the oppressed. . . . I am Hammu-rabi, the Just King, to whom Shamesh has granted the truth. My words are choice, my deeds have no rival; only for the unwise are they vain, for the profoundly wise they are worthy of all praise" (translated in Driver and Miles, 1955:97-99).

Yet, even in these worthy words, bias is not altogether absent in the resolution of conflicts. True to the form of preindustrial hierarchical societies, the code distinguishes the rights of free men, citizens, and slaves. Law eight, for example, states that the thief of an ox or a sheep or an ass or a swine or a boat should repay the owner thirtyfold if it is the property of a palace or "god," tenfold if it is the property of a "villein," and, if the thief cannot afford repayment, that he should be put to death (Driver and Miles, 1955:17). Similarly, laws 196 to 205 distinguish punishments for injury on the basis of status. If a man put out the eye of a free man, his eye was to have been put out in turn; if he broke the bone of a free man, his bone should also have been broken. However, should he have put out the eye or broken the bone of a "villein," he was able to repay him with silver; and should he similarly have injured a free man's slave, he was to have paid restitution of half his price. Should a man have struck the cheek of a free man superior in rank, he was supposed to have been beaten before an assembly sixty times with an ox-hide whip (pp. 78-79). Capital punishment, by burning, impalement, or drowning, was prescribed for a number of offenses, among them theft or possession of palace treasures (law six, p. 15).

A more suggestive indication of possible Babylonian inequity comes from the mythological character of the sanction Mesopotamian rulers apparently sought for their positions. Their power is said to have been derived from Enlil, a god who symbolized the option of compulsion by force. Under his authority, opposing wills are supposed to have been crushed into submission. Hammurabi's identification of Enlil's son, Sin, as his father, "stressed the terroristic quality of [his] position" (Wittfogel, 1957:138).

Hebrews

The source on ancient Hebrew government recounts both ideology and its breach: in the Old Testament, there *is* evidence of despotism. Whether or not it was in evidence in Judah under Josiah, the space and time pinpointed in the standard sample, must be inferred, however, from descriptions of earlier reigns.

The kingdom against which Samuel and the Deuteronomist (Deuteronomy 17:14-20) warned arose under David; under his son, proverbially wise Solomon, evidences of exploitation are recorded. Solomon "excelled all the kings of the earth in riches and wisdom" (1 Kings 10:23); he evidently was wise enough to enjoy the spoils of his father's conquests in tribute and staggering amounts of forced labor (e.g., 1 Kings 9:15-23). He was able to impress the Queen of Sheba with the palace he had had built, the food of his table which, in contrast to the limited consumption of meat during special occasions among the rural population, included a daily spread of large quantities of cattle (Noth, 1958:212), and the attendance of his servants, of whom his horsemen alone numbered twelve thousand (1 Kings 10:5, 26). When Solomon died, "all the assembly of Israel" came with Jeroboam to say to Rehoboam, his son, "Your father made our yoke heavy. Now therefore lighten the hard service of your father and his heavy yoke upon us, and we will serve you" (1 Kings 12:4). Following the council of his peers, Rehoboam responded: "My father made your yoke heavy, but I will add to your yoke; my father chastised you with whips, but I will chastise you with scorpions" (1 Kings 12:14).

The single specific example in the Old Testament of the exercise of despotic exploitation comes, however, from the reign of Ahab (871-852 B.C.), roughly fifty years later. The case of Naboth's vineyard foreshadows the form of exploitations to come. Ahab initially offered to buy Naboth's vineyard, which bordered near his palace, and was refused. In response, his infamous wife, Jezebel, wrote letters in his name asking elders to "set two base fellows opposite him, and let them bring a charge against him, saying 'You have cursed God and the King.' Then take him out and stone him to death" (1 Kings 21:9-10). They did as they were told. "And so soon as Ahab heard that Naboth was dead, Ahab arose to go down to the vineyard of Naboth the Jezreelite, to take possession of it" (1 Kings 21:16).

In a summary of Hebrew justice, DeVaux (1961:159-160) noted that capital punishment was prescribed for idolatry (Exodous 22:19; Leviticus 20:1-5; Deuteronomy 13:2-19; 17:2-7), blasphemy (Leviticus 24:15-16), and profanation of the sabbath (Exodous 31:14-15; Numbers 15:32-36). In addition, a man who disobeyed an order of extermination and one who was guilty of lese-majesty were stoned (Josiah 7:25). The punishment could be increased by the exposure of the bodies, which were "hung on the gibbet," and taken down by nightfall (Deuteronomy 21:22-23). Like those of Dahomean offenders, the corpses of the guilty were probably impaled (Numbers 25:4 and 2 Samuel 9). In addition, there were prisons, in which the accused were kept awaiting a decision, and suspects were shut up by police action, "often arbitrarily" (DeVaux, 1961:160). Besides the confiscation of the estates of those condemned to death, evidenced in Naboth's case, and possibly a general sovereign right (Noth, 1958:214), the fact that arbiters are repeatedly warned against bribery throughout the Old Testament (see DeVaux, 1961:153) indicates that some of them enjoyed this perquisite as well.

Again, though, what is the evidence of despotism during Josiah's reign? The very short-lived sovereignty Josiah was able to reestablish for the kingdom of Judah in the decline of Assyrian power is not detailed in any of these respects. Of Manasseh, his grandfather, it is written that "he shed very much innocent blood, till he had filled Jerusalem from one end to the other" (2 Kings 21:16); however, Josiah "did what was right in the eyes of the Lord" (2 Kings 22:2). He was able to come fairly close to achieving his goal of reuniting Israel and Judah, and was even able to occupy territory which had not belonged to the kingdoms of David and Solomon, before being killed in 609 B.C. as Egypt expanded under Neco, twenty-two years before Jerusalem fell (Noth, 1958:274). To what extent this revival of power was paralleled by despotic exploitation must remain a matter for speculation.

Imperial Romans

In the second century A.D., the focal period in the standard sample, Romans enjoyed successive reigns of the "good emperors," Trajan, the focal emperor, among them. They were preceded immediately by Domitian's "reign of terror," which purged Rome of actual and imagined enemies of state, and earlier by the likes of Gaius Caligula, who, according to Suetonius, treated diners to displays of inquisition by torture, condemned to the beasts men of high rank innocent of any grave offense, and, according to Seneca, disposed of his quastor and other senators and knights by torture, "not to extract information, but to satisfy an inclination" (quoted in Garnsey, 1970:130, 144). They were succeeded immediately by Commodus, and eventually by centuries of arbitrary rule in Constantinople. At the gladiatorial games, Commodus is said to have staged a personal demonstration of despotic impulse for the benefit of Dio Cassius and other senators. "Having killed an ostrich and cut off its head, he came up to where we were sitting, holding the head in his left hand and in his right hand raising aloft his bloody sword; and though he spoke not a word, yet he wagged his head with a grin, indicating that he would treats us in the same way" (quoted in Starr, 1971:180). Nevertheless, according to Edward Gibbon, "If a man were called to fix the period in the history of the world during which the condition of the human race was most happy and prosperous, he would, without hesitation, name that which elapsed from the death of Domitian to the accession of Commodus" (from "Decline and Fall," quoted in Starr, 1971:124).

Correspondence between Trajan and Pliny the Younger support such a suggestion, indicating an intention to serve the interests of the governed. Following Nerva, who followed Domitian, Trajan swore not to abuse members of the senate with misuse of the law of *maiestras*, or treason. It was broadly defined to include conspiracies and plots, less serious but still treasonable acts, and treasonable words (Garnsey, 1970:107), and, since Augustus, adultery with a princess of the royal house (p. 45, 21). The penalty for *maiestras* was death.

A more striking example of Trajan's concern for his subjects was his extension of support to children of the poor. Grants were made to local landowners, and the interest appropriated for the maintenance of the indigent. Five thousand children are guessed to have benefitted by this form of welfare in Trajan's time (Balsdon, 1969:89). Although "the motive of the emperor was probably, as his panegyrist suggests, political as much as benevolent," possibly to encourage the rearing of children who would serve in state armies, as well as to stimulate agriculture (Dill, 1925:192), the results are sufficient to suggest that Roman subjects were not always injured under Imperial government. "The difficulty arises when we compare the high tone of the world which Pliny has immortalised, with the hideous revelations of contemporary license in the same class which meet us in Juvenal, Martial, and Tacitus" (p. 142).

Some indication of the capacity of Roman patricians of the second century to be arbitrary comes from evidence of their treatment of slaves. This is hardly exceptional; being frequently drawn from among the conquered, slaves are often by definition disenfranchized members of even the simplest societies. In Rome, however, the institution flourished to a notable extent; the Roman populace became itself predominantly of slave descent; and masters enjoyed an exercise of absolute power over their spectacular numbers. Tens of thousands of slaves were used as "articulate tools" on Roman farms and in the mines; at gladiatorial shows they were routinely killed as a form of entertainment; and even "talented and responsible" slaves were liable to suffer from "cruel caprice or normal disciplinary practices" in the households of senators and knights (Hopkins, 1978:119). In one case, according to a letter by Pliny the Younger, every slave in the household of the consul Afranius Dexter was put to death on their master's being found dead, of unknown cause, on the grounds that they were accessories after the crime for having endeavored inadequately to prevent it. "Roman slavery was a cruel system of extreme exploitation" (p. 131).

Even at the height of the Imperial period, there is evidence that such asymmetry extended to the emperor's relations with the enfranchised as well. Cicero recognized three forces which adversely affected the working of the law: *oratia*, or the favor of status, *potentia*, or the influence of power, and *pecunia,* or the bribery made possible by wealth (cited in Garnsey, 1970:207). Peter Garnsey, in his book "Social Status and Legal Privilege in the Roman Empire" (1970), explores the thesis that, even at its least despotic, Roman "justice" invariably incorporated Roman concepts of status. In general, the impeachment of defendants of high status by plaintiffs of low status was impeded both by the aristocratic biases of praetors and judges, and by the *de facto* inability of members of the lower classes, through lack of education and funds, to initiate legal proceedings (p. 218). On the other hand, low-status defendants, on being brought before the Senate or the Emperor, received harsher punishments than did high-status defendants for the same offense (p. 100). Garnsey says:

> The most serious penalty for offenders of low status was *summum supplicum.* This covered several aggravated forms of the death penalty, including exposure to wild beasts (*bestiis dari*), crucifixion (*crux*), and burning alive (*vivus uri, or crematio*). Condemnation to live and fight as a gladiator would normally involve the death of the condemned (at some juncture). *Metallum* was a life sentence to hard labour in the mines. A less grave penalty of the same type was *opus publicum,* or labour on public works and services. Corporal punishment was applied to *humiliores.* Torture traditionally was reserved for slaves, but free men of low rank were not immune in the second and third centuries (p. 104).

For high-status offenders, however, execution was rare; standard penalties were *deportatio* and *relegatio,* two forms of exile, and *motio ordine,* or expulsion from the senate, if the offender was a senator, or from the local council, if he was a decurion. When the emperor Justinian, two centuries later and hundreds of miles to the east, finally codified Roman law, it clearly incorporated the concept that status should mitigate punishment (Bury, 1923:413).

Lozi

Almost two millennia later and a continent distant, Gluckman addressed himself to the judicial processes among the Barotse of southern Africa. By the time of his investigation, the existence of British protectorate power and the Northern Rhodesian High Court for Appeals had restrained the king and his councillors from arbitrary acts. Previously, however, they may occasionally have been more capricious. Sorcery trials once punished individuals that Europeans might have considered innocent. Punishments were previously far harsher. And, according to early administrators, only very poor men, and those who would be useless as slaves, were killed for offenses, while the matter was dropped when it was considered "politic to do so" (Gluckman, 1972:218, 211).

A Lozi king formerly had been supposed to take action only through his officials, so that they could be held responsible for carrying out his instructions. If sued, they were not allowed to plead that they were acting for the monarch in their own defense. "If he does, he is accused of an offence, 'working,' or 'spoiling' the king's name, for which he can be severely punished . . . . *The king can do no wrong*" (Gluckman, 1965:34; emphasis added). Nonetheless, acknowledging that "Africa has had its Caligulas and Neros, as well as its Aureliuses and Antonines," Gluckman maintained that, with the exception of an early king "raised in foreign parts" who ate people and eventually was drowned by his councillors, only one out of eight other Barotse monarchs prior to the British conquest was said to have been a general tyrant. "Most kings are praised for their kindness to all people" (1965:48).

The conclusions of contemporaries of those kings is somewhat different. According to Bertrand (1899), Lewanika, the Barotse king at the turn of the century, and his elder sister, the Mokwai, were "representatives of the most complete absolutism. The land, and all that it contains, including the inhabitants, belongs to them by principle, and not one of their subjects is free in his actions" (p. 154; cf. p. 273). Prior to the arrival of missionaries, Barotse land might be referred to as a "land of blood" (p. 153). The king himself represented the courts of justice, appeal, and cassation (p. 273). Over those relatively underprivileged before the law, bias in the execution of "justice" was extreme. "For a mere nothing, a delay, an order ill executed, or an utensil broken, the servant, slave, or child will have his throat squeezed by his master's hands until he falls to the ground unconscious. Sometimes the victim does not come to life again" (p. 276). A "malefactor" would be found and placed in the path of warrior ants to be eaten alive. Despotic acts were not restricted to the lower classes; the Mokwai was reported a few years earlier to have killed with her own hand one of her elder dignitaries who had failed to "satisfy" her (p. 150).

Although the perquisites accruing to a Barotse authority for arbitration are only fleetingly mentioned (Gluckman, 1972:221), his privilege in tribute and labor was characteristically great. According to Gluckman, Barotse legends emphasize that "the kingship was established by people who themselves undertook the obligation to render tribute" (1965:29-30). If so, there is evidence here for substantial self-sacrifice. All wild animals killed, all honey, and the fat of all hippopotami, were supposed to revert by right to the king. A specified number of canoes, cattle, spears, axes, hoes, fish, skins, and stores of grain were by obligation given up to him every year. Lewanika's fields, which covered the country, were cultivated by forced laborers. Barotse chiefs from top to bottom of the social scale had the right to levy such labor, and the workers were bound to abandon whatever tasks they had undertaken for themselves to undertake the work of their leaders, from whom they could claim neither payment nor food. Forced laborers performed as messengers, boatmen, fishermen, porters, reapers, "&c., &c." (p. 274). The king and Mokwai were entitled to receive annually a number of children, of both sexes, to become their servants (Bertrand, 1899:154-155). The children of ruling Barotse alone were exempt from servitude. Finally, also characteristically, all subjects owed their monarch deference, including the obligation of squatting on their heels and clapping their hands at his entrance (p. 74). This standard difference in posture biased the ability of each, of course, to mount spontaneous displays of force.

Bemba

Historical perspective also appears to color Richards' account of the Bemba, also of southern Africa. She suggests that "a reputation for generosity and a system by which advancement could only be attained through royal favor naturally bound people" to the king (1940:106). However, the presence of a number of mutilated survivors of the old regime (Slaski [1950:91] commented on the number of natives, even court officials, with mutilated ears and hands) prompted her acknowledgment that much of their power also may have depended on force. Informants explained that the royal family were named after the crocodile because "they are like crocodiles that seize hold of the common people and tear them to bits with their teeth" (Richards, 1940:106).

According to Gouldsbury and Sharpe, disobedience of the Bemba king's orders, and failure to contribute the customary dues or labor, was "checked by mutilation, devastation of gardens, seizure of cattle, and, finally—for the contumacious—enslavery of the whole village to the Arab merchants who flocked around the capital" (1911:21). Crimes against the king included high treason, tried by an ordeal; even when it failed to find the accused guilty, he was kept under strict watch and deprived of chiefly powers, while his chief supporters were arrested and sold into slavery. Consistent with concerns of heads of state across cultures, crimes against the Bemba king also included adultery with his wives. Whether this involved actual cuckoldry or merely undue intimacy, the "luckless Lothario" was executed, and the woman subjected to mutilation (p. 55). On the other hand, all members of the royal family were considered above the law. Sons of royal blood, who had gone too far in their abuse of power, would be admonished with a proverb: " 'I shall veil my eyes with a goatskin'—as a hint that he would punish his offending relative with blind equity of justice. And actually, there are many cases of banishment [sic] on record" (p. 50). The statement by a turn of century British administrator that, tired of the atrocities of their chiefs, the Awemba welcomed British rule, is not hard to understand (pp. 21-22).

Mbundu

For the Mbundu and Suku of southwestern Africa, evidence of legal privilege by authority is less abundant than for other societies. Hambly, however, succinctly sums up Mbundu asymmetries: "The penalties for offences against the king were undoubtedly more severe than those imposed for the same offences against a commoner" (1934:202). The king's court was the supreme court in the nation where cases were tried and "fines eaten" (Childs, 1949:22). Any marked success by an individual would often result in his being tried for sorcery. Should the results of such success be widely shared, suspicion was less likely to arise. Persons convicted of such an offense might be banished; if the sentence was pronounced by a chief, it could be one of capital punishment (McCulloch, 1952:39-40). In addition, adultery with the wife of the king was punished by castration, although that punishment could be commuted to a very large payment, while the guilty and his sisters and sister's sons would become slaves of the king (Hambly, 1934:203). Nevertheless, according to Childs, among legitimate kings of Ovimbundu there were "comparatively" few "revolting and wholesale punishments" (1949:21).

Suku

Similarly, only the option to exploit is brought up in Kopytoff's retrospective on Suku conflict resolution (1961). Formally, the king acted as supreme judge in the settling of disputes; regionally, local chiefs held those powers. According to Torday and Joyce, the only exception to a pecuniary punishment among a nearby tribe was for treason, for which the penalty was death (1906:48). "The Ba-Yaka are ruled by one great chief called Muri Kongo, who considers them all his slaves; on entering his presence all prostrate themselves and beat their breasts. His power is absolute" (p. 44).

Fur

In the Sudan, in Fur society, deference was again paid to authority. The sultan would appear with half his face veiled, "and it was counted the height of offensiveness for any of his subjects, even his chief men, to look at him straight in the face" (MacMichael, 1922:114). One properly addressed him half kneeling and half sitting, with head bowed and eyes abased. According to Beaton, the *Magdums* of the older sultanate had powers of life and death over their subjects, while chiefs were left other criminal cases to arbitrate (1948:7). Ali Dinai, whose government from 1899-1916 was "one of centralization and cruelty" (p. 5), reserved for himself the right to pronounce a sentence of death. "The last of the sultans is variously credited with clubbing murderers to death, beating to a pulp inefficient tax collectors, lopping off the hands of thieves and castrating adulterers" (p. 7). The greatest evidence of advantage to Fur authorities, however, comes from accounts of perquisites connected with arbitration. "The spring of justice was in fact a revenue-producing item in the budget. . . . Whatever the division of the spoils, the purpose was to fill the purses of the sultan, courtiers, viceroys, chief and steward. Under such a system it paid everyone, except the guilty, for court business to be brisk and for the heaviest fines to be imposed" (p. 8).

Samoans

After years of foreign contact, Turner in 1884 made the following generalization about Samoan government past and present. "The government had, and still has, more of the patriarchal and democratic in it, than of the monarchical" (p. 173). Nevertheless, he noted that Samoans had always had commonly understood penalties for offenses such as theft, adultery, murder, and injury, as well as other "minor" offenses, such as disrespectful language to a chief, and that "the further back we go in their history we find their punishments were all the more severe" (p. 178). Exiles might have their houses burned and plantations taken from them; fines in quantities sufficient to provide feasts for entire villages were common (pp. 178-179). Severe punishments of prior days included forms of public humiliation, the likes of which served as deterrent exhibitions of force in most despotic groups. Among them, a man's hands might be tied behind his back as he was paraded naked in daylight; he might be made to sit nude in the South Pacific sun, hung up by his heels, or asked to play handball with a sea urchin (pp. 179-180).

Stair (1897) modified the view of Samoan government as a democracy: "Until a comparatively recent period, the government of Samoa appears to have approached more nearly to that of Tahiti and the Sandwich Islands, which is monarchical, than would be supposed from its present condition" (p. 76). The government of earlier chiefs, however, had vanished with the right to inhabit abandoned, massive raised stone platforms "which seem to have been the work of an earlier but now extinct race of men" (p. 112). Stair supposed that the power of chiefs formerly varied, often being very limited, but, by chiefs of highest rank, being frequently used in a tyrannical manner (p. 70). Powerful advisors are said to have banished chiefs on account of their excessive tyranny and oppression. Like Tikopians, Samoan offenders of a chief were obliged to prostrate themselves on hands and knees, with their heads between the latter, before his house, awaiting a decision. "It occasionally happened that the injured parties were unable to control their passions on seeing this enemy prostrate before them, in which case they rushed out spear and club in hand to inflict summary chastisement upon the humbled company" (p. 97).

In his recent recapitulation of evidence on Samoan society, Freeman (1983) notes that a variety of harsh punishments was once administered, "particularly for acts of disobedience or disrespect to chiefs" (p. 195). One extreme castigation involved tying the offender up like a pig, making an oven to symbolize his being about to be "cooked," and forcing him to ingest human excrement, an apparent porcine habit. These ultimate forms of subjugation were "meted out to anyone who cast aspersions on the genealogy of the chief" (p. 193). Quite surprisingly, Freeman notes that a prosecution for such a punishment, *saisai*, was heard in the Supreme Court of Western Samoa as late as 1981.

Natchez

Few hierarchical societies arose in the Americas, but those that did appear to have been true to the general form. In the lower Mississippi valley, the word despotism is almost invariably used in early accounts of the government of the Natchez chief. According to DuPratz, he was "absolute master of the goods and life of his subjects," disposing of them at his pleasure; "his will is his reason" (quoted in Swanton, 1911:106). According to Charlevoix, the relationship between a chief and his subjects could be characterized almost as slavery; as soon as anyone had the misfortune to displease either the Sun or the woman most closely related to him, they were ordered to be killed by guards. "Go and rid me of that dog" they would say, and be immediately obeyed (in Swanton, 1911:101). The authority of the great chief extended to his relatives in proportion to their nearness in blood (DuPratz, in Swanton, 1911:106).

Although specific information on the collection of legislative perquisites is absent, there is evidence of the general privilege of the Natchez hierarchy head. His house is said to have been sufficiently large to have held four thousand (Penicaut, in Swanton, 1911:100); according to Charlevoix, subjects were obligated to carry him the best of their hunting, fishing and harvests; Le Petit says that they were compelled to carry out his labors on command, and were forbidden to exact any wages (in Swanton, 1911:101, 103). Whenever he spoke, his subjects honored him by howling nine times; they similarly howled upon approaching him, which they could not do nearer than four paces, and upon retiring, which they were obliged to do walking backward (Charlevoix, in Swanton, 1911:101-102). Upon paying a visit to his "cabin," "those who enter salute by a howl, and advance even to the bottom of the cabin without looking at the right side where the chief is. Then they give a new salute by raising their arms above the head and howling three times. If it be anyone whom the chief holds in consideration he answers by a slight sigh and makes a sign to him to be seated" (Le Petit, in Swanton, 1911:102). Following every question the chief puts, he is obliged to howl again, and when he leaves, he prolongs his howl until he is out of his presence. Apropos, chiefs and nobles were distinguished from subjects by the labels "Suns and Honored men," and "Stinkards" (Dumont, in Swanton, 1911:103).

Azande

In the Nilotic Sudan, Lagae asked of the Azande: "How many times in the past has a whole clan been exterminated in a chiefdom for a crime of lese-majesty of one of the members, or because of adultery with the wife of the chief!" (1926:32). Casati said of one Zande chief, Bakangoi, "Death was the punishment he inflicted for the least fault." A sentence was commuted only in exceptional cases, "to persons of the upper classes, never to the people" (1891:199). Where chiefs saw fit to show such leniency, they evidently often received a Darwinian compensation in the form of women. According to Brock, in one case a man was made to pay three women in compensation to a chief for killing his dog (1918:252). According to Czekanowski, such women were specifically to be those "capable of producing sons" (1924:52; emphasis added).

According to Baxter and Butt, the principal delicts tried by Zande chiefs consisted of offenses against their absolute authority, including disloyalty, using magic against them, committing adultery with one of their wives, or participating in an organization which usurped chiefly functions. "These offenses, in which a chief was personally concerned, were settled summarily by a chief in his own interest. Charges which were clearly true . . . were seldom settled at a properly constituted court but were settled immediately by the chiefs, and the penalty formerly was usually instant strangulation at the hands of the chief himself or his bodyguard. The chief's judgment was never questioned" (1953:55).

When the penalty of death for adultery with the wife of a chief was mitigated, offenders were emasculated, and in addition, their hands, ears, and lips were cut off. "One still comes across these unfortunate men, very often in the train of the chief" (Brock, 1918:258). Even when the penalty of death was enforced, the relatives of the adulterer had to pay several women in indemnity to the chief. Sometimes, they were themselves reduced to slavery (Lagae, 1926:24). At the other extreme of social privilege, when the offended husband in an adultery matter was not an aristocratic Avungara, the adulterer could atone for his transgressions by making "a present of cloth, or beads, or spears" (Reynolds, 1904:241). Mutilation, at least, was also inflicted by authority for refusing to obey a call to arms, cowardice in the face of an enemy, and neglecting to pay tribute to a chief (Anderson, 1911:243-4).

Like Roman patricians, Avungara used the law to conserve their privilege. "Avungara were almost above the law and the poison oracle as applied to commoners" (Baxter and Butt, 1953:59). This was in part because they could be chastised or punished by their superiors only, and in part because commoners were deterred from making accusations against members of the upper class. They put the names of their "betters" before the oracle only at a risk to themselves; "their lives would be a misery if they insulted the most important men in their neighborhood." Should an oracle prove a commoner innocent of an accusation made by an Avungara, no indemnity would be paid; he was to have considered himself fortunate that his innocence was acknowledged. But should the oracle prove an Avungara innocent of a commoner's accusation, the accuser was immediately put to death (Huttereau, 1909:29). Thus, "The poison oracle acted as a conservative force, which buttressed the social order at every point" (Baxter and Butt, 1953:59).

Kafa

The Kafa of Ethiopia disposed of those guilty of rebellion and treason by hanging. Typically, "treason" was broadly defined, including wearing gold ornaments without permission of the king, eating fowl if female, and eating cabbage if male and a member of the Minjo clan. Witchcraft and lycanthropy, in this case, nocturnal transmutation into a hyena, also warranted the death penalty, and families of the guilty were enslaved (Huntingford, 1955:126). According to Huntingford, any ill-disposed individual was liable to make an accusation of lycanthropy before the king's council. "This led to much injustice." The justice of the last king, Gaki Seroco, is said to have been notoriously summary and cruel, "executions were frequent, and . . . any breach of ceremonial concerning the king was punished with death" (p. 126). The king had the power of life and death over his subjects (p. 116); according to a Kafa maxim, "The king is the law" (p. 125).

The people were properly in awe of it. When the king went out, "everyone tried to hide or threw themselves on the ground when he passed so that their faces were concealed;" they feared even his glance (p. 116). The person of a monarch could not be touched. And, those bold enough to have made requests of him did so in fully prostrate position, with both arms stretched out before them. However, his subjects owed him more than deference.

His privilege was proportionate. Typically, the king had the right to demand labor for any purpose from any except the warrior clan. Peasants were obliged to cultivate the king's land under the direction of his provincial governors (p. 122). His revenue came from tribute in the form of a land tax in cattle paid by those who occupied it, from customs dues paid at the kingdom gates, and from fines. In addition, the bribing of judges was taken for granted to such an extent that, systematically, "a proportion of what they received in bribes went to the king, and formed a distinct source of revenue" (p. 125). The wealth he himself accrued as a result is evidenced, in part, by the description of his person. This was topped by a crown, *tate uko*, witnessed by Bieber; it was almost three feet high, and "consisted of a conical head-piece to which was attached in front a triple phallus of gold; the head-piece was ornamented with gold and silver plates, and a row of silver chains hung down from the sides and back. From the apex of the head-piece an ostrich feather was held upright by a highly ornamented narrow holder. This crown was sacred" (Huntingford, 1955:118). The king's regalia also included golden earrings, a gold armlet, ring, and neckchain, a gold-wired silver staff, a golden sword, two golden shields, and a long green cloak and parasol. No one but the manarch could wear green and only he and his sub-kings were allowed to wear gold (p. 118).

Fijians

Williams (1884) painted a different picture of Fijian monarchy: on the frontispiece of his ethnography is the image of Thakombau, king of Mbau, reclining in perfect half-naked repose behind his fan. Evidently, his duties allowed him abundant leisure (p. 20). He apparently had earned his reprieve in characteristic fashion, by the awed servitude of his otherwise occupied subjects. His will, once again, was law (Waterhouse, 1866:337).

Lest they risk making an affront, the approach of his subjects was always "fulsomely respectful" (p. 338). Such behavior was enforced: "Fijians have been slain for disrespectful approach to chiefs" (p. 341). The conduct of the father of Thakombau, Tanoa, is said to have been especially awe inspiring; he killed and cannibalized slaves and possibly other subjects without any provocation whatsoever (p. 56). On the other hand, it was tabu for a commoner to lift a club against a noble (p. 99). Williams (1884) sums up the attitude of Fijian authority.

> No actual provision is made for the security of the life and possessions of the subject, who is regarded merely as property, and his welfare but seldom considered. Acts of oppression are common. The views of the chiefs do not accord with those of the wise son of Sirach, for they are not "ashamed to take away a portion or a gift," but will not only seize the presents made to an inferior, but, in some cases, appropriate what a plebeian has received in payment for work done. So far from being condemned as mean and shameful, it is considered chief-like! (p. 18).

A number of examples of such actions are cited, including the case of the chief who requested a hoe from a subject and, on being refused, took his wife instead; the case of the Mbau chief who, on finding his villagers had cut him fewer reeds than he wanted, had the village burned; and the case of the mere petty chief who, discovering that a man had accidentally injured one of his ducks, supposing it wild, demanded the fingers of four individuals in compensation, and shut the culprit up with the duck, insisting that he might live only on condition of saving the bird (pp. 20-24). In general, "Offences, in Fijian estimation, are light or grave according to the rank of the offender. Murder by a chief is less heinous than a petty larceny committed by a man of low rank" (p. 22).

Again, liberal tribute was ceded to Mbau authority, including the best of the gardens, seines, and sties in Fiji, "together with compliments the most extravagant and Oriental in their form" (p. 31). In addition, subjects gave their labor, when asked, in peace, and of course their service in war. According to Williams, much of this was returned (1884:33); nevertheless, the rights of chiefs to what they demanded was unquestioned; and a chief could take anything from a common man (p. 281). Finally, chiefs collected perquisites in connection with the resolution of conflicts. Like Otoro, they acted as accomplices after the fact in cases of theft; on condition of being given a part of what was stolen, they made no prosecution (Waterhouse, 1886:331). In the punishment of offenders, chiefs confiscated the property of their kinsmen, appropriated some of their female relatives, and/or killed some members of their tribes (p. 329).

Ashanti

The wealth reaped by litigation, however, may have reached a culmination in the practice of African Gold Coast Ashanti law. The *Ashante Hene*, king of Ashanti, and great paramount chiefs alone had the right to pass a sentence of death. Alternatively, the king might demand blood money, or *atitodie*; the whole amount of the *atitodie* belonged to the king (Rattray, 1929:185, 161). He would accept it with the benediction, "I present you with your head." The *atitodie* was "limited" to the greatest amount the accused and his clan could be expected to collect, "and might necessitate the selling of whole villages with their inhabitants in order to raise money" (Rattray, 1927:209). An *innocent* party, on the other hand, was compelled to pay *aseda*, or a "thank offering" that he had gotten away with his life. This was a fixed and comparatively small amount, and was divided among court officials and servants, members of the public present at the trial, the queen mother and women of the blood, and the children and grandchildren of the chief (Rattray, 1929:115). While *atitodie* could amount to as much as £800 at the time of Rattray's writing, the maximum *aseda* was approximately £6 13s. In addition, certain capital offenses were punished with forfeiture, although care was taken not to seize the property of family members not involved in the crime (Rattray, 1923:227). The results of the netting of such great sums as the proceeds of litigation was, not exceptionally, that they came to represent an important means of replenishing a depleted treasury. "Prayers were offered to the gods to send cases" (Rattray, 1929:292).

Capital crimes in Ashanti, as elsewhere, consisted largely of personal offenses against authority. They included invoking a spirit to kill the king, "blessing" (cursing) the king and his ancestors, and committing adultery with any of his many wives, or with any woman of the (royal) blood (Rattray, 1923:131). Cowardice before an enemy, and the tasting of first fruits before they had been presented to authority, also could merit a punishment of death (Rattray, 1929:126; 249). Commission of relatively pedestrian offenses, such as theft, upon the person or property of kings also became a capital offense (Rattray, 1929:311). The most striking deterrent display of punishment came, again not surprisingly, in the event that a man had been bold enough to contract a liaison with a member of the king's harem. In this event, the mother, father, and maternal uncle of both parties were killed, and their remaining relatives had to "drink the gods" in swearing that they were not complicitors in the crime. The guilty wife was beheaded; the guilty man was asked to dance the "dance of death."

> The culprit, through whose cheeks a sepow knife has already been thrust, is taken, about six o'clock in the morning. . . . The nasal septum is now pierced, and through the aperture is threaded a thorny creeper, called kokora, by which he is later led about. Four other sepow knives are now thrust through various parts of his body, care being taken not to press them so deeply as to wound any vital spot. He is now led by the rope

creeper . . . to Akyeremade, where the chief of that stool would scrape his left leg, facetiously remarking as he did so . . . "I am scraping perfume for my wives;" next to the house of the chief of Asafo, where his left ear is cut off; thence to Bantama, . . . where the Ashanti generalissimo . . . scrapes bare the right shin bone; then the man is taken back beneath the shade of the atopere tree. Here he is compelled to dance all day. . . . After dark, . . . his arms are now hacked off at the elbows, and his legs below the knee; then his eyelids are cut off. He is ordered to continue dancing, but as he is unable to do so, his buttocks are sliced off and he is set on a little pile of gunpowder which is set alight. . . . The chief executioner now reports to the king that the man is nearly dead, and receives permission to cut off his head (Rattray, 1927:88-89).

Finally, although any commoner might initiate proceedings to de-stool a chief, he did so only at great personal risk. Should such a man, for example, "one whose wife the chief may have seduced" decide to undertake such action, he must rally public support against the chief, compelling the elders to hold a trial. If the accused was unable to "prove" his case, he would, in the old days, almost certainly have been killed. However, should the chief be found guilty, he might be given another, or even two more, chances (Rattray, 1929:145-146). Plotting to destool a chief "without just cause" was, of course, considered treason, a capital offense (p. 312).

Ganda

Arbitrariness may find its apotheosis in the Ganda case. Speke (1864) describes the capricious Ganda king, dressed in red, walking down the road, his men before him and women behind, occasionally firing his rifle off. Happening upon a woman awaiting punishment for an un-known cause, he stops to mingle "a little business with pleasure," taking the trouble to act the executioner on impulse (p. 361). According to Kagwa (1934), young men who ill behaved themselves by littering the streets of the capitol or falling in love with princesses were liable to wholesale slaughter. Occasionally, their offenses were not so auda-cious; they were killed at the whim of a fortune teller who decreed that all persons with cataracts or white hands or other heinous traits should immediately be put to death. Accordingly, the king would send his policemen out to arrest all those concerned, "and sometimes even some not concerned" (p. 80). Some with the ability to amuse him the king exempted from such trouble, including flutists, trumpeters, butlers, doorkeepers, cooks, and others; these carried the marks of their trade. Any others upon whose persons such symbols were lacking were liable, when the almighty had decreed it, to be "brutally beaten or even murdered without cause. . . . The number killed on any such occasion varied from one or a few up to several hundred" (p. 81).

Occasionally, a man's relatives might petition for mercy from the sovereign. Should they be so fortunate as to catch him in one of his better tempers, and happen to have brought along two or three good looking girls with which to beg his pardon, they might succeed in staying his hand (Kagwa, 1934:81). Speke cites an example of the striking of one such bargain; men sent to die were relieved of the penalty by the payment of "fines of cattle and young damsels—their daughters" (1864:358). A king evidently benefitted by fining to a considerable extent. Chiefs failing to perform their duties to his satisfaction could be assessed up to 100 women, 100 cattle, and 100 bundles of barkcloth, to be paid within fifteen days! (Kagwa, 1934:97).

Evidently, bribery was sufficiently rife throughout the courts that a system of symbolic communication pertaining to such perquisites sprang up. A defendant could promise a judge a slave by rubbing his hand on his head, a cow by putting his fist to the side of his face to resemble a horn, a load of barkcloths by pulling at his own clothes, and a woman by clenching his fist on his breast (Roscoe, 1911:261). Even those payments made by peasants for offenses against one another were great. If one committed adultery with the other's wife, he was obliged to repay him ten cows, ten goats, ten loads of barkcloth, and ten women. However, he paid only part of this fine, leaving the rest unpaid for years, waiting to be let off the hook by bringing a charge against the other man in turn, or relying upon time to heal the wound. On the other hand, "If a peasant found that his chief was making love to his wife, he would pack up his goods and leave the district by night lest he should be put to death on her account; should his wife refuse to go with him, he would leave her behind" (Roscoe, 1911:262-264). For so much as casting his eye for a minute on a woman of the palace, a man gave his life (Speke, 1864:326-327).

Khmer

When, in thirteenth century southeast Asia, the Khmer king proceeded forth from his palace, he wore a crown of gold, gold bracelets, anklets, and rings, and carried a golden sword; more than three pounds of large pearls hung from his neck. He was preceded first by the palace girls, bearing burdens of gold and silver, and then by gold-ornamented carriages, and more than a hundred gilded parasols and twenty white parasols garnished with gold. The king followed standing on an elephant with gold-covered tusks, or carried by four of the palace girls on a golden palanquin (Briggs, 1951:250). The powers of the king were limited only "by his conscience and tradition" (Thompson, 1927:331). Inequality before the law was the rule; guilt was determined by rank (p. 330; cf. Aymonier, 1900:103).

Those of his subjects unfortunate enough to have been found guilty were likely to have found their punishments most unpleasant. Prior to the revisions made in 1624, a slow death could be brought on in any of twenty-one ways, appendages could be mutilated, and "extraordinary refinements of cruelty" awaited the individual convicted of treason against country, religion, or the king. Even after the seventeenth century liberalization, "Today those condemned to death are decapitated, strangled, shot, pierced with spears, occasionally given up to the elephants" (Aymonier, 1900:103). Aymonier also discusses in the present tense the use of vises on temples and ankles, blows with a stick or leather switches, and flagellation with dried buffalo hide or lashes of rattan, the yoking of criminals to plows in the fields, and the tormenting of them with dozens of tiny arrows while they are tied in a public market (p. 105). Pecuniary punishments included confiscation in full or in part of the criminal's property, along with, for increasing offenses, that of his wife, his children, and all of his relations. Fines, proportionate to damage done and social condition, were given in two parts to judges and court criers, in four parts to the victim, and in four parts to the royal treasury (p. 106). "As in medieval Europe royal justice has used the court of appeal to back the local power of the feudality, and to fill the treasury with revenues" (Thompson, 1927:331).

Aztecs

Aztec rulers apparently took pains to prevent injustice. If they suspected ill of their judges, that they delayed the cases of commoners, or considered kinship or bribes in pronouncing judgment, they "jailed them in wooden cages, exacted the penalty, and slew them, so that the judge might walk in dread" (Sahagun, 1951b:42). Sahagun's informants insist that judges were selected for their praiseworthy attention to justice. "Such as these the ruler gave office and chose as his judges—the wise, the able, the sage . . . who did nothing for friendship's or kinship's sake, nor for enmity; who would not hear nor judge a case for a fee" (p. 54).

On the other hand, Aztec law was severe. Although Etzalqualitzli, as servants of the idols, were entitled to rob those they passed on the road, beat resisters and leave them for dead, with impunity (Sahagun, 1951a:11), slanderers had their lips and sometimes their ears cut off, and impersonators of high officials, witches, market and highway robbers, and thieves of the silver, gold, and precious stones reserved for religious ornaments, were all put to death (Vaillant, 1941:120-121). Cuicacalli, overseers of young men's work and leisure, found guilty of an offense such as drunkenness, concubinage, or seeking personal advantage in governance behind the ruler's back, as by levying tribute without his permission, were strangled, stoned, or beaten to death. And theft by a majordomo from the tribute cache similarly brought on a capital penalty, in which case his property went to the king. "Thus the ruler implanted fear" (Sahagun, 1951b:43-44).

Sahagun paints a picture in stark contrast to Speke's (1864) of the Ganda king, of an Aztec ruler passing along the public road. "If any poor vassal, who made bold to hail the ruler, greeted him pleasingly, then the ruler commanded the majordomo to give him a cape, a breech clout, and a place for him to sleep," as well as food and drink to meet his needs. In particular, "If some poor indigent were to fashion or to make so many skin drums, or a song of honor, if then he dedicated them to the ruler . . . , he enriched him" (1951b:59). Kings making their way in public might not, though, have been easily approached. When the ruler went forth, "his chamberlains and his elders went before him; on both sides, on either hand, they proceeded as they went clearing the way for him. None might cross in front of him; none might come before him; none might look up at him; none might come face to face with him" (p. 29).

Evidently, Aztec kings were particularly fond of song and dance, and frequently sponsored them to lighten subjects' spirits. On such occasions, they would outfit themselves in sprays of quetzal feathers and gold, with turquoise ornaments, and quetzal feather fans. "With a priceless cape he covered and wrapped himself, and in a costly breech clout he girt himself" (p. 56, cf. chapter 9, exclusively devoted to what the king wore when he danced). Once again, though, recollections of the glorious are tempered by suggestions of imperious heavy handedness. The unfortunate performer who failed to amuse was not kept on long. "If the singers did something amiss—perchance a two-toned drum was out of tune, or a ground drum; or he who intoned, marred the song; or the leader marred the dance—then the ruler commanded that they place in jail whoever had done the wrong; they imprisoned him, and he died" (ibid.).

Inca

And in conclusion, Garcilaso de la Vega's panegyric of Peruvian New World government: "It is certain that these King Yncas took extreme care to adminster equal justice, according to the laws of nature, to small and great, poor and rich alike, so that none could receive injury. They were beloved by the Indians for their rectitude and up-rightness, and their memory will be revered for many ages by the people" (1871:493). The harshness of the punishments they used to execute justice he acknowledged, but deemed wise, as the severe infliction of the penalties of the law "and the natural love of life and hatred of death in men" led to an avoidance of crimes which resulted in death (p. 147).

Penalties included public rebuke, loss of office, exile, the Hiwaya, torture, imprisonment, and death. In the Hiwaya, a large stone was dropped from nearly three feet up onto the criminal's back, often bringing about his death. Otherwise, stoning, hanging by the feet, throwing from a cliff, or beating the head in with a club brought on a similar end. Imprisonment, inflicted only upon those guilty of the most perfidious forms of treason, also amounted to execution, as the criminal was put into an underground dungeon to compete for his life against puma, jaguars, vultures, snakes, and other carnivores. Again, the essential determinant of punishment was rank. Inca law "held that public ridicule and loss of office hurt a noble as much as exile or torture would a poor man, and that the prestige of nobles as a class must be upheld" (Rowe, 1946:271).

Torts against authority were treated, again, particularly harshly. One was not to curse the king, or the queen, or "the sun or the moon or the idols of resplendent gold," under pain of extermination (Pomo de Ayala, 1936:180); the phrase, "Our father the Sun" was not to pass the lips of those not of Inca blood, lest the blasphemer be stoned (Garcilaso de la Vega, 1871:63-64). As a form of tribute, natives from specific villages, on a rotating basis, offered their services at the palace. They acted as sweepers, water bearers, wood cutters, cooks, and courtiers; they filled almost every conceivable function. They probably served extremely well: any offense they committed against the monarch was looked on as an offense committed by their village; accordingly, in punishment, the village was leveled to the ground. "These employments were much prized among the Indians, as they enabled them to be nearer the royal person, which was an honour they most esteemed" (Garcilaso de la Vega, 1871:773-774).

Finally, for violation of the women of the Ynca, or of the Sun, the law directed that the culprit's wife, children, servants, and relatives, as well as all the inhabitants of his village and all their flocks, should be put to death "without leaving a suckling nor a crying baby, as the saying is" (p. 298). The village was to be pulled down and the site strewn with stones, "that the birthplace of so bad a son might for ever remain desolate and accursed, where no man nor even beast might rest" (pp. 298-301). "All was truth and good and justice and law" (Pomo de Ayala, 1936:326).

According to Garcilaso, this was true to such an extent that no subject ever risked breaking the law, while the Inca of royal blood was inca-

pable of committing such a breach. How could he? Any act he perpe-
trated against a subject would have to have been, by definition, within
the law.

> If he happened to desire some pretty woman, the Inca knew that he had
> only to ask her father, who not only would not refuse to let him have her,
> but would also consider this opportunity to give satisfaction to his sover-
> eign as a great honor and good fortune. And the same thing was true with
> regard to material possession as to women, since the entire land belonged
> to the Sun and to his descendants, whether they occupied public office or
> not; this permitted them to choose whatever they wanted, throughout the
> Empire, without it being possible to refuse them; nor was there any more
> possibility that they might kill or wound someone than that they would
> take something from him, since the entire people adored them, and could
> not offend them, however slightly, without laying themselves open to the
> terrible punishments provided by the law (1961:25).

DISCUSSION

Of the twelve *preindustrial* societies in this sample with maximum
four-level jurisdictional hierarchies (Appendix II), there is some suggestion of despotism in all of them. In three cases, the evidence that
heads of hierarchies murdered their subjects for trivial or no cause is
not altogether conclusive. A systematic bias according to status in the
resolution of conflicts is manifest in Hammurabi's eighteenth century
B.C. Babylonian code; in addition, Hammurabi's choice of a god rep-
resenting compulsion by force as his paternal symbol further suggests
a possible proclivity toward exploitation. Nevertheless, in this case, no
explicit evidence of despotism exists. Similarly, although status, again,
systematically biased Roman legal decisions, and although Trajan is
supposed to have been surrounded on both sides by emperors guilty of
often grotesque abuses, the evidence his panegyricist, Pliny, copiously
penned does not play up Trajan's abuse of power. Finally, too little
evidence exists to draw any clear conclusion in the Suku case. Still,
what does exist again suggests the possibility of despotism: characteristically, a related king is said to have considered all of his subjects his
slaves. Under the remaining nine four-level preindustrial hierarchies,
the ethnographic and historical evidence leaves relatively little doubt
that leadership was in fact despotic. In five of the preindustrial societies
in the sample with three-level hierarchies, the Azande, Fijian, Samoan,
Natchez, and Aztec, despotism is in evidence as well; in two more, the
Mbundu and Hebrew cases, some suggestion of despotism also exists.
In no group with a lower-level hierarchy was leadership determined to
have been despotic.

The conclusion, in other words, seems consistent: men with great power do, as Lord Acton suggested, tend to exploit it. Consistent with the Darwinian hypothesis, hierarchical power is a good predictor of the extent to which individuals are able to bias conflicts in their own interests. In extreme cases, in preindustrial societies, they have murdered their subjects more or less arbitrarily with, of course, complete impunity.

In the last century, two major literatures have come to bear more or less directly on despotism. The first concerns the broad problem of conflict resolution; the second has always been explicitly concerned with the practical problem of ending exploitation. They are, first, comparative theories of "law," and, second, the Marxist tradition. The mass of each is as substantial as its subject matter. The discussion which follows is meant no more than to introduce the conspicuous points of intersection of each with the work done here. Each alternative both concurs and jars with a Darwinian interpretation.

Let the reader be warned. One of the most central trends in anthropological evidence and theory over the last century has been an increasing acknowledgment that self-interest is evident in all societies. Accordingly, the clearest alternatives to Darwinian theory are generally the oldest. Much recent comparative work on "law" and some new work done in the Marxist tradition has stressed that strength is an important determinant of the outcome of conflicts in any group, and that exploitation may be, sadly, in evidence to some extent in even the smallest societies. As all of the alternatives grow more consistent with the accumulating evidence, initial differences dissolve. One clear difference remains: Darwinian theory alone predicts that reproductive behavior will follow from the way in which conflicts of interest are resolved.

Theories of Conflict Resolution

In 1895, Emile Durkheim wrote that understanding individual behavior is irrelevant to understanding society. In the preface to the second edition of "The Rules of Sociological Method," he insisted to his critics that a man's control over his social order is less than obvious. "In vain have repeated experiences taught him that this omnipotence, the illusion of which he complacently entertains, has always been a cause of weakness in him; that his power over things really began only when he recognized that they have a nature of their own, and resigned himself to learning this nature from them" [1895 (1966):lviii; contrast Alexander, 1979:82-86]. A raison d'etre for the science of society was to be that understanding individual motivation would be inadequate, if not irrelevant, to account for social phenomena, including law.

According to Durkheim, in "mechanically integrated," essentially, preindustrial societies, "it is the assembly of the people which renders justice" [1893 (1933):76], not to an acting individual's advantage (p. 86), but to penalize offenses against the collective consciousness (p. 80). In this case, "Despotism, at least when it is not a pathological, decadent phenomenon, is nothing else than transformed communism" (p. 196).

Many subsequent theorists have similarly stressed the social function of conflict resolution. For instance, Malinowski, whose ethnographic interest in "law" was pioneering, suggested that its essential objective in Trobriand Island society was "to ensure a type of cooperation which is based on mutual concessions and sacrifices for a common end" [1926 (1982):64, cf. pp. 92–93]. More recently, in a comparative review of "primitive" law, Hoebel, although he acknowledged the existence of societies with "invidious law systems," defined law "not as an instrument of exploitation" (1954:327), but as "the creative consequence of a people's efforts to achieve and maintain a self-limiting order" (p. 326).

It is, of course, the democratic ideal that the "law" should be constituted by men of equal strength in greater numbers. For Roscoe Pound, for example, law is that ideal. "Many today say that law is power, where we used to think of it as a restraint upon power. . . . The legal order as a highly specialized form of social control rests upon the power or force of politically organized society. But so far from the law being power, it is something that organizes and systematizes the exercise of power and makes power effective toward the maintaining and furthering of civilization" (1942:49). In fact, though, the "law" has been historically laid down by men of greater force. This is consistent with the Darwinian prediction: any sanction for or against an action is likely to reflect the interests of those able to administer it. It is, of course, possible that strength in numbers might come to exceed the strength of any one individual and that the distribution of power might grow so equitable that the interests of a majority would generally overrule those of a minority. But historically, power has often been distributed quite inequitably; accordingly, "society," as a utilitarian majority, has not usually been the "law's" beneficiary.

This conclusion is increasingly in evidence in the cross-cultural literature on conflict resolution. It might be argued that it was anticipated in Maine's (1864) decision that in early "law," offenses, including murder and theft, were more often considered to have been committed against individuals, rather than against society. "If therefore the criterion of a delict, wrong, or tort be that the person who suffers it, and not the State, is considered to be wronged, it may be asserted that in the infancy of jurisprudence the citizen depends for protection against violence or fraud not on the Law of Crime but the Law of Tort" (p. 359).

This is especially true as in preindustrial groups trespass against the social welfare and the ruler's welfare were generally considered to be one and the same. Other writers, either reluctant to lack a theory of individual motivation (e.g., Ehrlich, 1936), or, in the Durkheimian tradition, explicitly rejecting the need of one (e.g., Black, 1976), have empirically determined that "law" is in fact related to power. But, without such a theory, they have been unable to explain their generalizations, or, except as a historical lesson, to offer predictions.

Many of the last generation of writers on the subject of early "law" have explicitly rejected an eclipsing focus on social over individual interests. Starr and Yngvesson, for example, have complained that "A Durkheimian emphasis on harmony of interests and shared goals has heavily influenced our thinking and seems to have shaped the ways in which anthropologists have perceived the handling of disputes. . . . A major problem of most anthropological dispute settlement studies is the failure to link status, rank, and class orientations to an understanding of actors' roles in, and outcomes of, the disputing process" (1975:559, 563; see also Pospisil, 1967:6). As members of a team of researchers sent into ten different cultures to address these problems, Starr and Yngvesson and several other students of Laura Nader confirmed that kinship, wealth, and status are generally among the most important determinants of conflict resolution (Nader and Todd, 1978). Introducing those findings, Nader and Todd admonished that "it is perhaps obvious to note that power and control over scarce resources are interconnected and relevant to disputing, and yet there has been little systematic discussion of law and the distribution of power in either the sociological or the anthropological literature. . . . We need to understand the processes whereby disputing mechanisms maintain and legitimize the distribution of power, and the means by which the powerful control disputing mechanisms" (pp. 19–20). In the last few years, a few prominent writers on law in preindustrial societies have begun in a tentative way to look at the possibility that a theory of evolved human motivation might yield predictions about and explanations of conflict resolution (e.g., Gruter and Bohannan, 1982, including Hoebel, 1982).

Marxism

On the subject of human society, the single most important alternative to Darwinism is probably Marxism. It is especially relevant to the subject of despotism, as the explicit end of Marxist thought has always been an end to exploitation.

Marxism and Darwinism have a great deal in common. It was in large part Darwin's work on organic evolution which inspired Marx's, and many others' including Morgan's (see Terray, 1972), attempts to come up with a parallel theory of social change. Social evolution, like biological evolution, was to be explicable in terms of changing historical conditions (e.g., discussion in Bloch, 1983). And for Marx, as for Darwin, the most important of those conditions were those which effected the ways in which people solved the material problems of life: production and reproduction. These parallels are fundamental. In order personally to acknowledge his debt, Marx originally proposed to dedicate "Capital" to Darwin (ibid).

In other crucial respects, though, the theories are far apart. The Darwinian hypotheses put forward here differ, first, from the Marxist insistence that the simplest human societies were without exploitation, second, from the Marxist emphasis on production, rather than reproduction, and, last but most importantly, from the Marxist prescription of a specific form of social evolution, socialist revolution.

The first difference, essentially, the idea of "primitive communism," derives from Marx and Engels' incorporation of the work of Lewis Henry Morgan into their scenario of world history. In his work on "Ancient Society" (1877), Morgan delineated two broad plans of government: *societas* and *civitas*. The first was founded on kinship, or more specifically, on clanship or gens, while the latter was based on territory, or property, and gave rise to the state. In gentile society, "The *state* did not exist. Their governments were essentially democratical" [Morgan, 1877 (1978):67]. Not only productive property, but reproductive rights, in husbands and wives, were supposed to have been held in common to varying degrees in gentile society. Only the growth of property was to have given rise to inequality, and made necessary a reorganization of society on the basis of territory (e.g., p. 215). To Morgan, it followed that "the element of property . . . has given mankind despotism, imperialism, monarchy, privileged classes, and finally representative democracy" (p. 342).

It might be important to speculate to what extent Morgan's idea that productive rights were once held communally was based upon his, and his contemporaries' (e.g., McLennan, 1865), idea that the earliest human societies were characterized by primitive promiscuity. For Morgan, in the "consanguine" family, inferred from a form of classificatory kinship terminology, for every man, "all my sisters are my wives, as well as the wives of my several brothers" (Morgan, 1877:410); husbands similarly, to at least some extent, were communally shared. To an even greater extent, he assumed, an earlier society might have practiced promiscuity. "The state of society indicated by the consanguine family points with logical directness to an anterior condition of promiscuous intercourse. There seems to be no escape from this conclusion, although questioned by so eminent a writer as Mr. Darwin" (pp. 417–418; cf. Darwin, 1871:893). The crucial extrapolation may have been that once reproductive rights were supposed to have been held in common, productive rights much more easily might have been supposed to have been shared. In Morgan's words, "Communism in living must, of necessity, have prevailed both in the consanguine and in the punaluan family, because it was a requirement of their condition" (p. 416).

Engels, after Marx's death, fit Morgan's conclusions to a Marxist interpretation. The initial stage of human society, in which property was supposed to be held communally and conjugal relationships to be characterized by promiscuity, was lifted whole from "Ancient Society." "And a wonderful constitution it is, this gentile constitution, in all its childlike simplicity. . . . All are equal and free—the women included" [1884 (1964):86]. Consistent with this rather romantic conception, the gentile constitution "possessed no means of coercion except public opinion" (p. 154; see also Bloch, 1983:60). A presumed fall from grace was attributed by Engels, as it had been by Morgan, to an increase in accumulable, heritable, wealth (especially pp. 144–153). Eventually, "The first attempt at forming a state consists in breaking up the gentes by dividing their members into those with privileges and those with none, and by further separating the latter into two productive classes and thus settling them one against the other" (p. 99).

A society free of exploitation was supposed to have been supplanted by the rise of social classes, one of which for the first time gained privileged access to the basic resources necessary to sustain life, while the other was cut off. Upon the heels of this change the state is supposed to have come into existence in order to preserve, by the use of force, the interests of the privileged class. The essential element in the Marxist conception of social evolution has therefore been that a sharp break occurred in history with the rise of the state; with this break, societies ceased to be "egalitarian," and exploitation and differential privilege emerged.

For the same reason that "primitive promiscuity," wherever common reproductive interest is insufficient to override individual interest, is incompatible with Darwinian theory, so is an absence of "private" property: both spouses and resources are means to reproductive ends. As individuals differ in their ability to attain them, having greater numbers of kinsmen or allies, more wealth, or any other edge, Darwinian theory predicts that they will differ in their access to them. Unlike the Marxist tradition, it predicts no sharp dichotomy in social relations; rather, to the extent that reproductive interests are not held in common, Darwinian theory predicts that individuals will exploit differences in strength wherever they exist.

A century of accumulated evidence about primitive society often has continued to be dichotomized into the "egalitarian" and "exploitive" forms of government originally delineated (e.g., Fried, 1967; references in Bloch, 1983). Recently, though, perhaps more in the spirit of Marx and Engels' original empiricism [e.g., 1845 (1976):31], some Marxist scholars have begun to suggest that no society has ever existed without classes. In, for example, an extensive review of Claude Meillassoux's (1964) Marxist analysis of Guro tribal economy, Emanuel Terray (1972) has been forced to defend an absence of class and exploitation in that society, following a contrary assertion by Georges Dupré and Pierre-Philippe Rey (n.d.), that "exploitation does . . . take place in traditional society" (Terray, 1972:167), and that classes therefore exist in such cases as well. A suggestion that some form of exploitation has been in evidence in even the smallest societies is consistent with the argument, and supporting evidence, here that conflicts of interest in all societies are resolved with a consistent bias in favor of men with greater power.

Other developing Marxist scenarios have begun to suggest a possible transition between classless and class society. An embryonic form of exploitation, or "Oriental despotism," is supposed by some to coincide with what Marx [1857–1858 (1973)] termed the "Asiatic" mode of production. Interest in this form of social relations, after a long dormancy phase, is being revived (see Dunn, 1982; Wittfogel, 1957; Krader, 1975; Godelier, 1978, 1981; Bailey and Llobera, 1981). The Asiatic mode of production was supposed to have been characteristic of societies in which property was owned communally, but in which production was often organized by a central bureaucracy. As Godelier has said, "This power at first takes root in functions of common interest . . . and, without ceasing to be a functional power, gradually transforms itself into an exploitative one" (1981:264). The view of despotism as a form of exploitation intermediate between primitive communism and capitalism may be somewhat problematic: the despotic practice of having subjects executed without pretext might be considered a form of "exploitation," though not, technically, the Marxist one, even greater than under some forms of capitalism. The point, though, is that developments softening the original dichotomy between exploitive and non-exploitive societies appear to bring Marxist theory closer to the facts.

Finally, that despotic power is in fact exploitive in the Marxist sense, that is, that the products of surplus labor are in fact appropriated (e.g., Terray, 1975:94), is highly likely. As Chagnon (1979a), again, has pointed out, at least some such surplus probably has to be appropriated to feed the families of reproductively successful men.

This brings up the second point of contrast between Marxism and Darwinism: the relative emphasis on production and reproduction. Again, for both, the essential determinant of social relations is the means by which individuals meet the objectives of producing and reproducing. The essential *difference* is that Darwinism is much more explicit: individuals have evolved to maximize their genetic representation in descendant generations. The relatively vague Marxist specification of motivation is common too to latter-day versions of historical materialism, including cultural materialism (see Harris, 1979:60–63). Marx and Engels were concerned with "the first premise of all human existence and, therefore, of all history, . . . that men must be in a position to live in order to be able to 'make history.' But life involves before everything else eating and drinking, housing, clothing, and various other things. The first historical act is thus the production of the means to satisfy these needs, the production of material life itself" [1845 (1976):41–42]. This is echoed later in Engels' assertion that, "according to the materialistic conception, the determining factor in history is, in the final instance, the production and reproduction of the immediate essentials of life[,] . . . on the one side, the production of the means of existence . . . , on the other side, the production of human beings themselves, the propagation of the species" [1884 (1964):5; cf. Engels, 1890].

This is obviously a close approximation of, but not identical to, the Darwinian prediction. The clearest difference between the theories remains that Marxism makes no explicit prediction that exploitation should coincide with the means to reproduction. It has been suggested that, in order to increase the plausibility of their prescriptions for a socialist society, Marx and Engels may have been reluctant to postulate any specific panhistorical human propensities (see, e.g., Venable, 1945; Masters, 1977, 1978; Bloch, 1983). But again, the unequivocal evidence that social relations *do* change with material conditions makes such a fiction unnecessary: novel forms of society continue to emerge with novel forms of industry. It is even possible that changing social relations by changing conditions might better be facilitated by an understanding of evolved motivations than by ignorance of them. Neither a Marxist theory acknowledging the historical absence of socialism, nor Darwinism, should preclude the possibility of future conditions under which individual interests might become common interests: under which individual welfare might best be served by serving the welfare of society (cf. Lewontin, Rose, and Kamin, 1984). *Neither theory precludes the possibility of the evolution of socialism.*

Finally is the last, and most important, point of contrast: Marxism is, above all, a prescription for socialism by revolution; Darwinian theory incorporates no prescription at all. Darwin declined Marx's "Capital" dedication because he was already "horrified . . . by the religious and political repercussions of what he had written" (Bloch, 1983:5). Nevertheless, again, even here the theories have more than is at first apparent in common: neither Darwinism nor Marxism precludes the possibility of the evolution of any form of human society.

> The fact is we are ignorant. We do not know the solution to such an elementary problem as singular or plural mates.
> —Leslie A. White (1949:335)

4

DIFFERENTIAL REPRODUCTION

It may be germane to begin again with an etymological point. Both *kin* and *king*, originally head of a gens, and *genius*, from the Latin, come from the Indo-European root, *gene*, "to beget." In other words, an association between power and powers of conception has not been unanticipated. In Rome, the snake symbolized the "genius," or fecundity, of the family father (Starr, 1971:46). In Israel, Absalom's taking his place publicly among his father's harem was tantamount to a claim to the throne (2 Samuel 16:21-22; De Vaux, 1961:116). Genius, generative power, kinship, and kingship evidently may long have been products of the same conception.

Even given that relatively complex societies may have been exceptionally successful at taking women from others, and that violent conflict both within and between such groups may have led to high male mortality, and so biased the adult sex ratio in favor of polygyny (see Spencer, 1876; Ember, 1974), the concentration of fertile women at the top of hierarchies would have necessitated a *relative* deprivation at the bottom, and so contributed to differential reproduction. The last, and most important question, remains: To what extent has despotism coincided with differential reproduction? Like Shinbone, and others with the portents of power, did despotic heads of state in fact seek reproductive advantage over their subjects in the numbers, nubility, and fidelity of their consorts? Again, in answer, the ethnographic evidence is adduced.

HAREMS

Dahomey is, again, a good point of departure. There, "in theory, all women were at the pleasure of the king" (Herskovits, 1938, v.2:45; emphasis added). Any object of his desire in female form, whether unmarried, married, or betrothed, could be taken away and added to the royal harem. "Fantastic accounts of the numbers of wives married to the potentate have been handed down; speaking in round numbers, the Dahomean informant ordinarily mentions several thousand" (ibid.). Consistent with this alleged sovereign right, a Dahomean man was supposed to refer to his wives as mothers, "no one being allowed to call them wives but the king" (Duncan, 1847:228). Besides the domestic variety, the king of Dahomey took his pick from among the women captured in war (Herskovits, 1938, v. 2:45).

Women of the Dahomean king's household were divided into four categories. First were the "wives," who were actually living with or had lived with the king. As Herskovits pointed out, their numbers precluded the equal right of each to full heterosexual relations. However, by keeping them in his harem, the king ensured his own reproductive success compared to the subjects he left without. This is an important point. To repeat: the number of women in such a harem may easily have prohibited the successful impregnation of each of them, but, their being kept from bearing children to others increased the monarch's relative reproductive accomplishment. In Dahomey, only some of the harem women were privileged to keep the king company continually; others had an opportunity to serve a potentially reproductive function by him only once or twice, or even not at all. For those, "the choice was celibacy or adultery," the latter only on pain of death (p. 45).

The second category of Dahomean palace women included the "Amazons," battalions of female warriors "who for some reason or other came under the control of the king, but whom he did not desire because of their lack of personal attractiveness" (p. 46). These too were expected to remain virgins, also on pain of death, while in the royal service. Nevertheless, Dahomeans were said to have "joked" that more soldiers may have died trying to scale the walls of the Amazons' quarters than at enemy hands; and Skertchey (1874:359–60) witnessed the collective punishment of eighty such offenders, a token four of whom were decapitated, the remainder being sent to the front. The third category of women of the king's household included female slaves; and the fourth was comprised of its elder women (Herskovits, 1938, v.2:46). A woman of the palace who had passed her youth might, if she had impressed the king, be kept on to perform a household task. "In the main, it was the younger, more attractive women who surrounded the king" (p. 45).

In Dahomey, and, as will be evident, in general, the reproductive hierarchy paralleled the social hierarchy. Many parents offered important chiefs their daughters in order to buy their favor; even village chiefs used their wealth and power to acquire and support more wives than could the village commoner (Herskovits, 1938, v. 1:339; v. 2:10). It is not surprising that the royal sib is said to have been "so large, indeed, that it had seemed as though in the city of Abomey at least, it would be difficult to find Dahomeans who were not descended from royalty" (v.2:38).

In Hammurabi's Babylon, the genius of kings has been intimated, but the number of their consorts not explicitly named. Marriage throughout Sumerian and Babylonian society was, as it has been (and remains) throughout European history, technically "monogamous," in the sense that a man might have only one socially recognized wife of equal status. "On the other hand, no stigma attached to resort to temple prostitutes or to the keeping of concubines," and a chief use, if not the sole function, of female slaves was concubinage (Saggs, 1962:185).

In ancient Israel, too, the evidence as to the exact size of Josiah's harem is sufficiently inadequate to require some reconstructive speculation. The most common form of marriage there and then was, typically, monogamy; however, royalty generally availed itself of the luxury of large numbers of concubines and wives (De Vaux, 1961:25). Like Solomon, the Deuteronomist warned the Israelites against their future king, that he might take too many wives (Deuteronomy 17:17). And the prophecy was again, in at least some instances, borne out. The king named in the Song of Songs had 60 queens and 80 concubines (Corinthians 6:8); David, even when his authority extended only over Hebron, had at least six wives (2 Samuel 3:2-5), and he later took more (2 Samuel 5:13, cf. 2 Samuel 19:6). Rehoboam, Solomon's ambitious son, is said to have had 60 concubines and 18 wives (2 Chronicles 11:21); however, Solomon's own success in this respect was apparently unsurpassed. "Now King Solomon loved many foreign women, together with the daugher of Pharaoh, women of the Moabites, Ammonites, Edomites, Sidonians, and Hittites. . . . And he had seven hundred wives, princesses, and three hundred concubines; and his wives turned away his heart" [1 Kings 11:1-3; cf. Twain, 1884 (1958):66]. But, the size of Josiah's harem remains a moot problem.

In second century Rome, Trajan, being a "good" emperor in a "monogamous" society, had only one legitimate wife, Plotina, and no legitimate heirs. Nor is it possible, in this case, to aver unequivocally that he, or any other emperor, enjoyed *de facto* polygyny in proportion to that of other monarchs. The capacity for extensive concubinage was, however, great. Rich Romans often took advantage of socially sanctioned concubinage, "but not a few thought even the light fetters of regular concubinage too rigid and too weighty. Preoccupied solely with their own ease and pleasure, . . . they held it preferable to rule as pashas over the slave harems which their riches permitted them to maintain" (Carcopino, 1940:102).

The numbers of slaves in residence from which such harems might be drawn were sometimes tremendously large. Wealthy Roman households with hundreds and even thousands of slaves are mentioned (e.g., Balsdon, 1969:107); by the third century, the imperial household included 1000 cooks, 1000 barbers, even more cupbearers, and "hives" of table servants and eunuchs (Friedlander, 1908:66). In Imperial Rome, the numbers of captive slaves grew to be sufficient to stimulate an extreme household division of labor. Every aristocratic exertion was spared by recourse to a slave (p. 219). They functioned, for example, as clocks, reminders of when to keep appointments, or even to go to bed. Seneca described a rich, uneducated man of the first century who used his slaves as cue cards at social functions. He had one memorize Homer, another Hesiod, and others the lyric poets, and had them prompt suitable quotations when the situations arose (cited in Friedlander, 1908:220).

Nevertheless, in an article called "Bastards in the Roman Aristocracy," Sir Ronald Syme (1960) admitted that, while the annals of Renaissance England, Italy, Spain, and France "proliferate" with illegitimates, in Rome, "there is a singluar dearth of evidence about aristocratic bastards. . . . It is not easy to produce an authentic bastard anywhere, let alone the bastard of a *nobilis*" (p. 323-324). Yet Augustus, according to Macrobius, once lightly asked of a provincial who resembled him whether his mother had ever been in Rome (and was answered, "No, but my father was"); the evidence is that Augustus and Claudius, at least, obligated their slave girls to become their mistresses by virtue of no more than their attraction to them; and Augustus' wife Seribonia's intolerance of those mistresses, her "moral perversity," was the ground on which he obtained a divorce (Balsdon, 1962:198, 230, 215). Some later emperors clearly enjoyed concubines in great numbers: Commodus is said to have had three hundred (Friedlander, 1908:64). In general, the Roman *nobilis* "was not in the habit of denying himself much, and opportunities abounded" (Syme, 1960:323).

How, then, account for the lack of Roman illegitimates? Syme suggests that, inheriting their mother's status, they simply followed them into social oblivion. "Here and there, no doubt, some freedman may have recalled by his physiognomy the dominant type of an aristocratic *gens*, and the clients whom the *nobiles* helped and promoted may sometimes have shared the ancestral blood" (p. 325). A recently asked question, "Why did the Romans free so many slaves?" (Hopkins, 1978:115), might be relevant in this connection. According to Hopkins, immense numbers of Roman slaves were freed. "The impression one gets from the sources is of a large number (i.e. tens of thousands) of ex-slaves mingled with the free-born in the city of Rome." Nor were they barred from attaining status on their own: a few amassed enviable fortunes, in at least one instance sixty times the minimum of a member of the senate, including 4000 slaves of his own; former slaves of emperors governed in the central Roman administration, and others were entrusted to govern provinces; and, in a debate in the Roman senate, many knights and even some senators were said to have been descended from former slaves (pp. 116-117). To Hopkins, the answer to his own question is that slaves were allowed, having excelled, to buy their freedom, at a price which made the arrangement profitable to both parties. Another possible reason may have been more intimately Darwinian: masters may have been freeing their children. This is consistent with a suggestion from Carcopino. As he pointed out, the "host" of epitaphs in which a husband saved a place in his tomb for his "freedmen" suggest that rich Romans may have been reserving places for their manumitted illegitimate sons (1940:102).

Back to nineteenth and twentieth century Africa. Gluckman, although he too offered no figures, noted that among the ruling south central African Lozi, "princes are very numerous for kings had many wives" (1965:30). This is reinforced by his statement that while a king's generosity was generally so much appreciated, the people resented his roving about the country, "and they disliked his habit of taking from his subjects those of their wives he desired" (p. 69). Missionary efforts to secure a coup in the conversion of King Lewanika were foiled, according to Bertrand, by his unwillingness to part with his harem (1899:72). Richards was a bit more specific about the size of central African Bemba harems; although commoners were, again, typically monogamous (some were fortunate enough to have taken a second or third wife), chiefs might have 10 to 15 women (1940:89), or, according to Whiteley, several dozen wives (1950:18). One Mbundu king of the southwest of Africa of the mid-nineteenth century, according to Childs, had 17 sons and 44 daughters; recent kings still had had as many as a dozen concubines and wives (1949:40). Although an estimated 80% of southwest African Suku marriages were monogamous around the turn of the century, important chiefs had "as many as ten or more" women, and

kings had close to forty wives (Kopytoff, 1965:452). Ethiopian Kafa
kings kept a number of concubines and up to nine "chief wives" (Gruhl,
1935:233). Finally, least explicitly, Felkin, not deigning to be quanti-
tative, referred to the "large harems of chiefs" among the Fur
(1885:234).

Turner (1884:96) wrote that chiefly Samoan brides at the end of the
last century brought along a brother's daughter or other "maid of
honour;" "hence, with his wife, a chief had one, two, or three concubines." In return, her relations received a share of evidently exemplary
mats, as "the more wives the chief wished to have, the better the heads
of families liked it, as every marriage was a fresh source of a fine mat
again. To such an extent was this carried on, that one match was hardly
over before another was in contemplation" (p. 176). By striking such
bargains, chiefs married up to fifty times. The number of wives any one
held concurrently remains subject to retrospective question; according
to Stair, once upon a time when polygyny was prevalent, high ranking
chiefs might have "seven or eight or even more *wives* at a time"
(1897:175; emphasis added).

Penicaut, again, suggested that the "cabin" of the Natchez Sun of the
Mississippi valley could hold as many as four thousand persons; Le
Petit mentioned "a number of beds on the left hand at entering;" but
neither suggested the size of his seraglio (quoted in Swanton, 1911:100,
102). Charlevoix added: Natchez "chiefs marry with less ceremony still
than others. It is enough for them to give notice to the relations of the
woman on whom they have cast their eye that they place her in the
numbers of their wives" (in Swanton, 1911:97).

Among turn of the century Azande, on the Nilotic Sudan, at even the
lowest levels of authority, commoner deputies took several wives and
became the heads of large families (Evans Pritchard, 1971:197). Ex-
pressing a by now taken for granted state of affairs, Lagae found that
although "it is true that every Zande aspires to be a polygamist . . . it is
no less true that polygyny remains the privilege of a small number"
(1926:160). The old census records of the Doruma territory revealed that
for every 100 adult men there were 26 bachelors, 47 monogamously
married, 18 married to 2 women, and 9 with more than 2 wives. Zande
chiefs had 30, 40 or even 100 wives (p. 160-163); and the king had more
than 500 women (Casati, 1891:198).

Again, Azande were attracted to and took to wife women with
substantial reproductive value. "Young women are often monoplized
by the rich polygamists, sometimes at eight years of age. Very often a
child of a few years is already paid for." Again, as the pattern began
among the likes of successful Tiwi and Nambicuara, this created a
difficulty for the less fortunate, who "must sometimes content them-

selves with the women whom the large polygamists no longer want"
(Lagae, 1926:179). Like Dahomean wives, Zande wives were divided
into four categories. The first two, "wives" of the chief, included the
nagbiya, literally, mother of the chief, who had the obligation of
watching over the harem, and the nagili, the preferred, and generally
idle, wives who, like the Nambikwara chief's favorites, followed him
about from place to place. The latter two categories were collectively
"slaves," women taken in war and given to the chief, with whom he
formally could not have relations, but whom he could at any time
elevate to the status of wife. They included the tibenagbiya, literally
those at the hand of the mother of the chief, and the tibeadiyabiya,
those at the disposal of the other of the chief's wives.

Mrs. Wallis visited Fiji in the first half of the nineteenth century,
during Tanoa's reign. She recalled that he once, "becoming quite
animated while enumerating the advantages of polygyny, said that he
had a hundred wives, and ended by advising my husband to get an
immediate supply" (1967:79-80). Toganivalu confirmed, "Tanoa had
many wives, ladies from various lands" (1912:1).

Back on the African Gold Coast, at the end of the nineteenth century,
according to Rattray, the number of wives of an Ashanti might vary from
two to a thousand. He footnoted that an earlier writer had attributed to
the King of Ashanti 3333 wives, but suggested he was mistaken to have
accepted as fact "a statement often heard but never intended to be taken
literally, this number being ascribed to him purely from a desire to flatter"
(1927:95). Such a figure, though artificially iterative, is not inconsistent
with the size of harems of potentates with similar power.

In eastern Africa, in 1875 Ganda, for example, the king filled his
enclosures with the women from whom he drew his wives; their
inferiors, mere important chiefs, kept hundreds of women in their own
enclosures (Roscoe, 1911:205, 10). Chiefs received gifts of girls, and
captured or were rewarded women in war. In addition, often when a
chief was told of an exceptionally stimulating young woman, "he
would send to her guardian, and tell him that he wished to marry her;
the guardian would then send the girl, and if the chief was pleased with
her, he would take her to wife," repaying her guardian with wealth.
Often they took prepubescent girls, keeping them tucked away in their
enclosures under the guardianship of older women "who kept them
from impropriety with men" (p. 93). Perhaps more directly, the Ganda
king "made a levy on the country for girls who in due course became his
wives" (p. 205). According to Kagwa (1934:68), landlords and chiefs
throughout the country held marriage councils, in which they selected
virgin girls between the ages of twelve and seventeen, from which they
presented the most attractive to the king.

In choosing his consorts from all of the women available to him, the monarch of Ganda evidently had the help of those who had already become his wives:

> The King's wives, when they saw a good-looking girl among their hand-maids, would bring her to the King, after having bathed her, and anointed her body with butter for several days, in order to make the skin soft. They would dress the girl in good barkcloths, and then pay the King a visit, pointing the girl out to him, and praising her; in this way they themselves would gain favour and receive presents from their lord; and the girl thus brought to the King's notice would be added to the numbers of his wives (Roscoe, 1911:87).

Although polygyny was in Ganda, as possibly everywhere else, the ideal: men generally aspired to it (e.g., Southwold, 1965:105), peasants seldom managed to have more than two or three wives, and the majority, as probably everywhere else, were fortunate to have one (Roscoe, 1911:95).

In 1292, in southeast Asia, the Khmer king had similarly stunning success in mating. He had just "five wives, one in his private apartment and one for each of the four cardinal points," but, in addition, "concubines and girls of the palace are estimated at three thousand to five thousand" (Briggs, 1951:245). The latter were subdivided into many classes; most of them never "crossed the threshold" of reproductive access to their king. Again, the sovereign right to the most attractive women of the kingdom obtained: "When a family has a beautiful daughter, it brings her to the palace" (p. 245). According to Aymonier, a new king inherited the entire harem of his predecessor, casting off women who no longer appealed. Although he was supposed to choose a queen to be grand mistress of his seraglio, he often preferred to confer titles on a handful of his favorite women, "who are placed above the multitude of concubines, actresses, dancers, musicians, singers, and all kept women" (1900:76).

In the New World, genius was no less apparent. Fragments of history remain in testimony to that of the Aztec kings. The Great Montezuma, for instance, "had many women as mistresses, daughters of Chieftains, and he had two great Cacias as his legitimate wives" (Diaz del Castillo, 1910:60). Bandelier (1880:613) cited the "dazzling polygyny" of Texcoco chiefs, one of whom, ironically, "Fasting Boy," was reported to have kept two thousand women.

Evidence of Inca powers of conception is more fully fleshed out. Peruvian kings kept their women in two cloisters, one for those of royal blood, destined to remain chaste as dedicated to the Sun, the other for the daughters of more distant kinswomen and commoners, chosen to be "concubines of the Ynca, but not of the Sun." Aristocratic Garcilaso, a descendant of Inca nobility, insisted that "their parents held it to be their greatest happiness to have the girls chosen as concubines of the King, as did the girls themselves" (Garcilaso de la Vega, 1871:299). Candidates for admission were not considered unless virgins of exceptional pulchritude, and, in order to secure the former condition, generally were not accepted over the age of eight. When the king required one, he was sent the loveliest to meet his needs (p. 300). "For there was no one of these lords who did not have more than seven hundred women for the service of his house and on whom to take his pleasure. Thus all of them had many children by these women who were their wives or concubines, and they were well treated by him and held in high regard by the natives" (Cieza de Leon, 1959:41). Houses of virgins available as concubines on the king's impulse were set up in principal provinces throughout the kingdom (Garcilaso de la Vega, 1871:299).

Those who were never given the opportunity to engage in reproductive activity remained chaste until they were old (probably, past the capacity of performing such a function), and were then given the opportunity to return to their homes (p. 301). Commoner concubines who did bear children transmitted to them their own lack of status; they were considered bastards, although respected as sons and daughters of the king. Besides these, kings had children by concubines related up to the fourth degree; these were considered to be of royal blood, and enjoyed proportionate privilege. Last, a king had children by his closest female relative, his legitimate wife; of these, the first born son was his legitimate heir (p. 310; for a Darwinian analysis of royal incest see Van den Berghe and Mesher, 1980).

In Inca Peru, reproductive rights apparently precisely paralleled political power by law. Caicques and "principal persons" were given fifty women "for their service and multiplying people in the kingdom." *Huno curaca* (leaders of vassal nations) were given thirty women; *guamanin apo* (heads of provinces of a hundred thousand) were allotted twenty women; *waranga curaca* (leaders of a thousand) got fifteen women; *piscapachaca* (administrators of five hundred) were allowed twelve women; *pacha camachicoc* (governors of a hundred) received eight women; *piscachuanga camachicoc* (petty chiefs over fifty men) were given seven women; *chunca camachicoc* (over ten) got five; *pichicamachicoc* (over five) got three; and the "poor Indian" took whatever was left! (Poma de Ayala, 1936:184). Higher offices were of course jealously guarded positions, available only to members of the Inca nobility (e.g., Karsten, 1949:99).

Rather before the fashion of Sun Yung Moon, the Inca king regulated the marriages of members of his royal lineage. Every year or two, girls of eighteen to twenty and young men not under twenty-four were gathered together in Cuzco, the capital city, to be wed. "The Inca placed himself in the midst of the contracting parties, who were arranged near each other, and, looking upon them, called the man and the woman to him, and . . . united them in the bond of matrimony" (Garcilaso de la Vega, 1871:306-307). These they were to consider their *legitimate* husbands and wives. "For nothing was so important to these Indians as women" (Polo de Ondegardo, 1916:102).

After very generously taking the time to review an early draft of these results, a reader remarked that they showed simply that powerful men like sex. This may be a necessary but insufficient conclusion. The capacity for sexual pleasure and propensity to seek sexual variety probably adhere to human males with some generality (see, e.g., Symons, 1979). It is a good bet that virtually all men like sex; powerful men may be most able to obtain it. An explanation of polygyny solely in terms of masculine desire for sex and sexual variety too fails to explain another general phenomenon: male sexual jealousy (see, e.g., Daly, Wilson, and Weghorst, 1982). Evidently, the wives and concubines of powerful men are almost invariably subject to some kind of seclusion.

CLAUSTRATION

In studying the determinants of the structure of primate societies, Richard Wrangham concluded that females organize themselves about subsistence resources, while males organize themselves about females (1979, 1980). Recent scenarios of hominid evolution generally conclude that a significant impetus differentiating humans from primate ancestors was the increased concession by males to contribute to parental care (Alexander and Noonan, 1979; Symons, 1979; Benshoof and Thornhill, 1979; Lovejoy, 1981; Strassmann, 1981; Allen et al., 1982; Turke, 1984b). To the extent that men have been willing to help rear children, the determinants of social organization may have been reversed. Although women retain by far the greater physiological mandate to invest in children by gestation and lactation, inasmuch as subsequent parental investment comes from fathers, men may have become the trackers of resources, including other men's labor, and women the trackers of the parental investment of men (cf. Emlen and Oring, 1977).

In striking the bargain for greater parental investment by a father, a mother must, again, increase his confidence of paternity (Trivers, 1972). To the extent that they are able to reciprocate with parental care, men may be in a position to demand increasing fidelity in their women by keeping them watched and hidden, as well as by severely punishing transgressions. This makes sense *if* sex serves the function of biological reproduction; if not, men have no apparent universal reason to so jealously protect against adultery by their wives (see Symons, 1979; Daly, Wilson, and Weghorst, 1982).

Mildred Dickemann in 1981 first explicated the facts of veiling and claustration in Darwinian terms. As she made clear, cases of female seclusion *do* correspond to hypergynous competition for high status, i.e., highly investing, males. Husbands, by supporting wife, children, and through inheritance, generations of grandchildren, are buying a higher probability of genetic paternity; the wives' families, by the payment of dowries and by guaranteeing their daughter's fidelity, are "purchasing increased probable reproductive success," for themselves, for her, and for her more probably polygynous, i.e., "sexy" (Weatherhead and Robertson, 1979), sons (Dickemann, 1981:428; see also Dickemann, 1979a).

Although an unfortunate proportion of ethnographers have not been concerned with the details of differential reproduction, including claustration, evidence of some form of harem seclusion exists for many despotic groups. In Dahomey, "The king's wives enjoyed extraordinary privileges;" in return, their approach was always signaled by the ringing of a bell by the woman servant or slave who invariably preceded them. "The moment this bell is heard all persons, whether male or female, turn their backs, but the males must retire to a certain distance. In passing through the town this is one of the most intolerable nuisances" (Herskovits, 1938, v. 2:35). When they were not about, all women of the royal house, including the Amazons, were "severely segregated from all men by their masters" (v. 1:339); they were not allowed to appear in the marketplace, and were seldom seen at all, except at occasional ceremonials, when the youngest and most attractive of them would be shown off (v. 2:48). In general, however, a Dahomean woman paid for her share, and her children's share, of the resources of her lord. "Once having entered the compound of the chief, she rarely leaves it, and is never allowed to go outside its walls unaccompanied" (v. 1:339).

Babylonian temple women occasionally lived in the *gagu*, or "cloister" complex of buildings in the temple precincts having its own administration and land (Saggs, 1962:350). As Dickemann (1981:430) points out in a review of Old World institutions of seculsion, evidence of claustration, in the form of a walled interior courtyard, exists for Babylonian Mari; and claustration in second storey rooms with latticed, narrow windows is mentioned in the Old Testament as well.

In many cases, elaborate fortifications erected for the purposes of defense may have served the dual (identical?) function of protecting the chastity of women of the harem. The Lozi king's residence was protected by a high palisade of reeds, from which an interior courtyard was accessible by a "narrow opening." Surrounding Lewanika's house was a harem of sturdily built round huts thirty feet in height. "Each hut is surrounded by a high palisade. Everything is very neat" (Bertrand, 1899:136).

Perhaps in a similar fashion lived the wives of a Bemba chief, "in huts fenced round by a common stockade" (Whiteley, 1950:18), and those of a Suku or a Kafa king. The Suku king's compound "was surrounded by a fence of bamboo and visitors had to be admitted by a guard. The compound contained the king's own house [and] those of his wives" (Kopytoff, 1965:460). And chiefly Kafa households were "surrounded by a large enclosure which no sick or deformed person might enter" (Huntingford, 1955:118); the king's residence was enclosed by a ten-foot high stockade, and at the palace, each of his wives had her own residence and servants' quarters (p. 118, 120).

Kafa women, like many kept in harems, were equipped with their own household and servants, and probably lived reasonably comfortably in most respects, except, like most women under such circumstances, for a lack of liberal masculine company. "The Imperial wives were subject to a specially severe control and even the courtesans dare not have intercourse with any other man than the Emperor" (Gruhl, 1935:233).

Azande apparently went to some lengths deliberately to deter breaches of chastity. The household of a chief and his harem was "generally in a place where no one can go without his authorization." It was always divided into three very distinct sections: a public quarter, a judicial quarter, and the private quarters of the chief and his consorts. It was always set on the thickly wooded banks of a river; sometimes, the river flowed between the public and private quarters. "We still find this custom of isolating the homestead and harem of the chief. Formerly, whoever passed this reserved place was punished by death" (Lagae, 1926:158-159). Only petty (female?) servants, and "inoffensive mutilated individuals" were allowed to enter the harem with relative freedom (p. 163).

As might be expected, consistent with their apparent pleasure in despotism and generous enjoyment of women, Ganda kings very circumspectly guarded against the possibility of cuckoldry. "Both the king and the chiefs exercised a certain amount of restraint over their wives" (Roscoe, 1911:93). At the capitol, houses were contained within an enclosure of high reed fences; wives were largely confined to the women's quarters located behind their husband's house, within which each lived separately, with her maids, in her own residence. No man entered these quarters without the husband's permission; the entrance to the women's quarters was guarded by a "trusted servant," who admitted trespassers on pain of death, or of "some terrible mutilation in the event of his life being spared" (p. 94). When the king's wives ventured forth from their seclusion, "the king's pages escorted them, chasing away anyone who remained on the road, or who tried to pass them. People were expected to cede the road to these ladies, and anyone failing to comply with the custom was severely handled by the pages; markets and houses were plundered by the pages as they went along, and the people thought themselves fortunate if they escaped with broken limbs" (p. 94). No woman was ever allowed out on her own; on their return, her escort was to report to her husband in detail what had transpired, including with whom his wife had been so bold as to converse.

Of the effective claustration of Khmer women, only an indication remains in evidence: "I have heard say that inside the palace are many marvelous places; but the defenses are very secure and it is impossible to enter" (Chou Ta-Kuan, quoted in Briggs, 1951:245). Similarly, there remain only suggestions of the possible seclusion of Aztec women, such as the mention that "Montezuma's [private] apartments . . . contained all the appurtenances of a sybaritic potentate [; and his] two wives and his many concubines occupied magnificent quarters" (Valliant, 1941:231). The capitol, Tenochtitlan, itself being situated on a lake, was a "natural fort" (p. 219).

Of Inca women, the picture is again more complete. Like the virgins dedicated to the Sun, of royal blood, those not of noble line kept throughout the kingdom were subject to the strictest claustration.

> They lived in perpetual seclusion to the end of their lives, and preseved their virginity; and they were not permitted to converse, or have inter-course with, or to see any man, nor any woman who was not one of themselves. For it was said that the women . . . should not be made common by being seen of any. . . . Among other arrangements in the house of the virgins, there was a narrow passage, admitting of only two people to walk abreast, which traversed the whole building. In this passage there were many recesses on either hand, which were used as offices where the women worked. At each door there was a careful portress, and in the last recess, at the end of the passage, were the women. . . . All things relating to them were in conformity with the life and conversation of women who observed perpetual seclusion and virginity (Garcilaso de la Vega, 1871:293-294, 298; cf. pp. 299-300).

The virgins dedicated to the Inca king's pleasure passed their days, weaving and sewing nobles' clothes, and making bread and liquor for their ceremonial consumption (p. 297-298), while "their needs were most abundantly furnished for" (p. 293). Once they had been called by their king to endeavor to serve their reproductive function, they could never again return to the house of virgins, but served as servants in the royal palace, until they obtained permission to be returned to their homes (p. 301). Again, in the event that they were never called, they waited out their lives in seclusion, until, in old age, they were given the option to go home. In the meantime, they were kept under the protective watch of the *mama-cunas* who ruled over them, making sure that should their master ever require a virgin, a virgin he would be sent.

DISCUSSION

In eight of the fourteen despotic societies in the sample, the head of the hierarchy's "wives" numbered more than a hundred. In four more groups for which specific information was found, the number of his simultaneous conjugal relationships ranged from eleven to a hundred; and for the remaining two groups, the Barotse and Fur, the qualitative suggestion is that leaders had, at least, "large harems." In general, heads of early states enjoyed privileged access to their subject's youngest and most attractive women, took them to wife and cloistered them, and, anecdotal evidence suggests, took their subjects' less secluded wives on clandestine occasions. Clearly, consistent with the Darwinian prediction, men who exploited their positions of power took proportionate reproductive rewards.

That women were actually valued for their ability to produce children is attested to in part by the fact that, cross-culturally, couples without children divorce more often (e.g., Ardener, 1962; Day, 1963; Cohen, 1971; Chester, 1977; National Center for Health Statistics, 1977; Thornton, 1977; United Nations, 1977; Reyna, 1979; see also Van den Berghe, 1979:47; Paige and Paige, 1981:203). In fertile unions, bride price installments frequently have followed the birth of children; when these unions nevertheless dissolved, bride price already paid often has been subtracted from the amount refunded for each child retained. "Bridewealth" therefore has been considered a misnomer; "child wealth" may be a more appropriate term (Goody, 1976:8; Van den Berghe, 1979:100). Interestingly, Paige and Paige (1981:202-206), in their study of standard sample tribal societies, found that their measures of "fraternal interest group strength," including the presence of stable and valuable economic resources controllable by adult men, the military defensibility of those resources, and patrilocality, all correlated positively and significantly with the ability of husbands to demand bridewealth compensation in the event of barrenness, infanticide, or abortion.

In the present sample, there is further evidence that a major function of marriage has been reproduction. Although the problem of causes of conjugal dissolution often is not delved into or even addressed in the ethnographies, explicit statements that sterility was considered such a cause were found in the authoritative accounts of 37 of the 104 sample societies. If other related factors, including impotence, sexual neglect, the death of children, too few children, and the wife's being too old to produce children, are included, accounts of at least 53, or just over half, of the sample societies list infertility as a cause for divorce. In others, a second wife is said to have been taken explicitly to fill the failed function of a childless first wife [e.g., Vreeland, 1954:52 (Khalka Mongols); Best, 1924:228 (Maori)], or, childlessness is said to have prompted adoption [e.g., Stair, 1897:178 (Samoans); Lambert, 1970:268 (Gilbertese); Birket-Smith and De Laguna, 1938:137 (Eyak)], probably of a close kinsman (Silk, 1980). Accounts of other groups mention that the birth of children strengthened the marriage tie [e.g., Porter, 1823:113 (Marquesans); Jenness, 1922:160 (Copper Eskimo); Bowers, 1965:110 (Hidatsa); Swanton, 1911:97 (Natchez); Huxley and Capa, 1964:73 (Amahuaca); Holmberg, 1960:83 (Siriono)], or that marriage was not considered consummated until children had been produced [e.g., Beaton, 1948:18 (Fur); Radcliffe-Brown, 1922:71 (Andamanese); Coon, 1950:24: Gheg). Finally, infertile wives often have been replaced by kinswomen [e.g., East, 1939:102 (Tiv); Seligman and Seligman, 1932:586 (Azande); Elmendorf, 1960:359 (Yurok)]; and, consistent with the inclusive fitness hypothesis (Hamilton, 1964), sterile husbands sometimes strove toward "vicarious paternity" (coined by G. P. Murdock for Filipovitch, 1958), by lending their wives to close kinsmen [e.g., Torday and Joyce, 1906:45 (Suku)]. Ethnographic accounts list infidelity by a wife as a cause for divorce in at least 48 sample societies; in others, more severe measures were taken to terminate the union. In no case is a husband's adultery listed as justification for severing the conjugal tie where the wife's infidelity did not merit her divorce or death (cf. Broude and Greene, 1976).

Like the conclusion that "powerful men like sex" (cf. Whiting, 1964), economic theories of the taking of a wife or wives may fail to explain several facts. Among them: husbands of sufficient means so often cloister their women; and women incapable of producing children by their husbands, as well as those having risked producing children by others, are frequently divorced.

One economic theory suggests that conjugal relationships stem from the sexual division of labor in effect in most societies, or more broadly from the economic value of women. Murdock (1949), for example, suggested that marriage, and the nuclear family deriving from it, fulfills sexual, economic, and reproductive functions. However, since the first

may be fulfilled outside of marriage, he argued that economic cooperation, based on the division of labor between men and women, may be
the necessary incentive for long-term conjugal association. Reproduction was thought to follow as a matter of course: "Sexual cohabitation
leads inevitably to the birth of offspring" (p. 9). In statistical tests using
cross-cultural data from the World Ethnographic Sample (Murdock,
1957), Ethnographic Atlas (Murdock, 1967), and standard sample
(Murdock and White, 1969), respectively, Heath (1958), Goody (1976,
see p. 129), and White, Burton, and Dow (1981) found a significant
correlation between a woman's contribution to subsistence activities
and the proportion of men married polygynously in a society (see also
Boserup, 1970). It is consistent with the Darwinian hypothesis that
where women contribute most to the household, polygyny may be a
feasibility for a larger group of men. However, that inability to reproduce and adultery on the part of the wife are significant causes of
conjugal dissolution, and that wives frequently are cloistered against
the possibility of infidelity, perhaps even to the detriment of their
ability to carry on economic activity, remain unaccounted for in the
theory that the economic value of women motivates polygyny.

A second body of economic theory suggests that polygyny maximizes
"utility" largely by the production of "economically" valuable children
(see Becker, 1981, especially pp. 52-53; Paige and Paige, 1981, e.g., pp.
43-46). This theory overlaps most closely with the Darwinian prediction, especially since "utility" is broadly defined, and may include
subjective tastes in addition to the products of labor (e.g., Becker, 1960,
1981; Easterlin, 1975; cf. the critique by Burling, 1962). Whether or not
children represent a net productive gain or loss remains a debated
question (e.g., Mueller, 1976; Cain, 1977; Caldwell, 1977; Nag, White,
and Peet, 1978; Vlassoff, 1982; Turke, 1984c, 1985). Like the labor
contribution of wives, that of children may make polygyny feasible for
a larger proportion of men in a given society. Although this economic
theory is consistent with the finding that infertility frequently prompts
divorce, it does not as clearly predict that a man should sequester his
wife away from other men, or kill or divorce her for producing an
"economically" valuable child by an unrelated man.

Neither economic theory clearly explains why men with means often
prefer to take prepubescent girls to wife. A Darwinian explanation
might be that the payoff for their early support may be the insurance of
their virginity. Virginity, better than any other indicator, may guarantee
that a young woman is not pregnant by another at the time of her
acquisition. On the other hand, an 8 year old's contribution to household economy is neither likely to be greater than her elder's, nor is the

probability of an early economic return in the form of children capable of making such a contribution increased.

Other theories suggest that polygyny may serve a political function (see Clignet, 1970), by cementing alliances with affinal and, given the union is fertile, genetic ties. Given, however, that infertile affinal ties frequently dissolve, or are reinforced by the substitution of another woman in hopes of producing children, the importance of the blood tie may be prominent in forging political bonds (see Fortes, 1959; cf. Leach, 1957, 1961). This suggests that a Darwinian explanation, kin selection (Hamilton, 1964), may in some measure account for the cross-cultural importance of politically motivated polygyny. As the evidence above amply suggests, political power in itself may be explained, at least in part, as providing a position from which to gain reproductively.

Finally, polygyny has been explained as serving a prestige function (see Stephens, 1963:53). This can be turned on its head quite easily: prestige may be understood to accrue to an individual in a position others aspire to; universally, men may aspire to polygyny. Although generosity and other characteristics often thought of as altruistic also frequently correlate with prestige, the individual who is generous to the point of exhausting his privilege may unfortunately not find himself rewarded by the greater admiration of his peers. Prestige, then, may more convincingly be seen as an effect of polygyny.

Many of the precise "proximate," physiological, means to reproductive ends have yet to be defined. However, the apparently very general propensities on the part of men to enjoy sex, to seek sexual variety, and to exhibit sexual jealousy are likely together to have advanced the cause of "genius" throughout evolutionary history, that is, to have ensured that men with means in fact have outreproduced those without. Again, this conclusion is hardly meant to sound like a paean. That powerful men have been reproductively successful hardly implies that they should be judged successful by any other criterion. In fact, in terms of Darwinian power to beget, most "Blessed be the unseen micro-organisms/For without doubt they shall inherit the earth" (Hecht, 1980:63).

As the power of men in authority grows with hierarchy, so does their right to their subjects' women, the number and youth of those in their harems, and their seclusion of them. Although an aggregate of theories may serve to explain these facts, they may most parsimoniously be accounted for by the simple Darwinian prediction that individuals have evolved to strive to maximize reproduction. To some extent, the exploitation in evidence in the resolution of conflicts of interest may also be explained by a collection of independently derived theories, including Marxism. On the other hand, the continuous, concurrent development of asymmetries in both despotism and degree of polygyny with hierarchy in preindustrial societies may best be understood as the sum of individual actions motivated toward differential reproduction.

> Shall quips and sentences and these paper bullets of the brain
> awe a man from the career of his humour? No; the world must
> be peopled.
> —Shakespeare *Much Ado About Nothing*, II, iii

5

SUMMARY

E volution was in the air a hundred years ago. But despite the fact
that the greatest writers on social structure, function, and change,
including Durkheim, Morgan, and Marx, owed and often openly acknowledged a debt to Darwin, there was no room for biology in any of
their philosophies. Organic evolution was adopted as analogy; and
anti-reductionism was, again, for many the *raison d'etre* for the "science" of society. Durkheim was probably most explicit about it; his
descendants and theirs have for generations stood behind that precedent. And they've been shooting paper bullets at biology ever since.

The evidence, though, suggests that a direct application of Darwin's
own theory and method might prove enormously useful after all. An
understanding that, unless common interest overrides individual interests, individuals should have evolved to exploit positions of
strength, answers the question of why power corrupts. It both predicts
and explains the near universality of despotic governments in hierarchical societies prior to the development of modern industry. And an
understanding that those able to win conflicts of interest should be
motivated, ultimately, to seek reproductive success, again both predicts
and explains the apparent universality of the nubility, fidelity, and
extraordinary numbers of a despot's concubines and wives.

These predictions have not gone untested in nonhuman groups.
Among the outstanding studies showing that winners of conflicts enjoy
more reproductive success are those of species as diverse as paper
wasps (e.g., West Eberhard, 1967, 1969), domestic chickens (e.g., Guhl
and Fischer, 1969), laboratory mice (De Fries and McClearn, 1970),
elephant seals (Le Boeuf, 1974), and red deer (Clutton-Brock, Guinness,

and Albon, 1982; all but the last are discussed in Wilson, 1975:Chapter 13). "The fundamental element in and basis for the definition of dominance is a stable asymmetry in the agonistic behavior of two or more animals." This in turn has often been shown to correlate with measures of successful reproduction, particularly in some taxonomic groups (Dewsbury, 1982).

The attempt to correlate rank, generally defined as an ability to displace other animals over a conflict of interest, with reproductive success, has been a central problem in primate studies. Studies of a variety of species assessing associations between measures of dominance and indicides of male mating success (including courtship length, consort number, copulatory rate, and, occasionally, genetic paternity tests), have yielded mixed results (recently reviewed in Fedigan, 1983).

The surprising thing is that, even though the hypothesis is completely contrary to so much contemporary common experience, the evidence here on preindustrial human societies may be more clear cut. Not only are men regularly able to win conflicts of interest more polygynous, but the degree of their polygyny is predictable from the degree of bias with which the conflicts are resolved. Despotism, defined as an exercised right to murder arbitrarily and with impunity, virtually invariably coincides with the greatest degree of polygyny, and presumably, with a correspondingly high degree of differential reproduction.

Again, even in societies with no formal hierarchy, conflicts of interest exist, consequent homicide rates may be arguably as high as in the modern United States, and the most often cited motives for violence among men involve women. To the winners, apparently, go the spoils. Men with relatively great accumulated strength win out, whether by their own physical prowess, or by alliances recruited by genetic relationship or an ability to reciprocate by payment. Where power differentials, and the bias in disputing outcomes, are smallest, successful men generally take no more than three or four wives at a time. As hierarchical power and bias increase, men take more wives, younger wives, and more faithful wives. They might even, in some cases, bias their investment in sons over daughters, and so, if their sons too are successful polygynists, successfully maximize their production of grandchildren.

In every preindustrial society in the sample with a complex hierarchy, some suggestion that leaders may have exercised despotic power over their subjects exists. In three cases, including the Babylonians under Hammurabi, the Romans under Trajan, and the Suku of central Africa, the evidence of despotism is implicating, but not completely incriminating.

Conclusive evidence of an exercised ability to kill subjects for trivial or no cause with impunity exists for every other four-level preindustrial hierarchy, and for many three-level jurisdictional hierarchies as well. The ability of kings to enforce their own interests in the event of a conflict gets to be extreme. The *Ashante Hene*, for instance, bade subjects adulterous with women in his harem to undergo the progressive mutilation called the "dance of death;" the Ganda king had hundreds of subjects at the capital killed for cataracts; Aztec kings slaughtered subjects who sang out of tune; and Inca "Suns," not at all unusually, had any blasphemers against royalty stoned. Under complex preindustrial hierarchies, despotism appears clearly to have been a general phenomenon. Insult was generally added to injury as winners of conflicts systematically took perquisites in connection with arbitration. This enterprise was, not uncommonly, so immensely profitable for the Ashanti that, eventually, "prayers were offered to the gods to send cases."

This conclusion is in some ways at odds with both theories of primitive "law," and with Marxism, most particularly with earlier versions of both. The Durkheimian notion that law was at first administered by an assembly of the people, to penalize offenses against the collective consciousness, and subsequent theories stressing the social function of conflict resolution, including Hoebel's, Malinowski's, and Pound's, have neither predicted nor explained why men in power consistently win disputes inequitably. Similarly, the finding of a consistent bias in the resolution of conflicts of interest in favor of the strongest, in every society, is inconsistent with the dichotomies of Morgan, Engels, Marx, and some modern Marxists, which insist upon an absence of exploitation in stateless groups. Darwinian theory, to the contrary, predicts that unless common interests are sufficient to eclipse individual conflicts of interest, people will everywhere exploit power to win those conflicts. The evidence strongly suggests that they do.

Last: do the winners reward themselves reproductively? Again, they certainly do. Consistent with the Darwinian prediction, the size of despot's harems reflects the degree of bias they effect in resolving conflicts. In four four-level preindustrial hierarchies, including the Lozi, the Fur, Babylonians, and Imperial Romans, no explicit numbers exist as to the size of emperors' harems. Nonetheless, in every case, a qualitative statement supports the prediction. For the Lozi, princes were said to have been numerous, because kings had had so many wives; and their subjects are said to have resented the royal practice of requisitioning any of their wives they desired. For the Fur, the bare statement that chiefs had "large harems" constitutes the last word on the subject. Babylonians, formally monogamous, had abundant use of concubines and slaves. Similarly, for jurally monogamous Imperial Romans, the option of socially sanctioned concubinage was open, as was, at least according to some historians, the option to rule over huge slave harems, taken from hoards of household slaves documented to have numbered into the thousands.

In every other despotic group, leaders are explicitly said to have enjoyed at least 10, more often over 100, and frequently over 1000, simultaneous conjugal unions. Conversely, harems of more than 100 are found in no group lacking despotic government. The evidence from well-documented cases is stunning. The Dahomean king, like the Lozi king, took his pick among his subjects' women; a Dahomean subject was in fact to refer to his wives as mothers, as no one had the right to call them wives but the king; altogether, subdivided into four different classes, the Dahomean king is said to have kept to himself "several thousand" women. The Khmer king kept five wives, one for the palace and another for each of the cardinal points, and 3000 to 5000 "girls of the palace" for his pleasure. In Inca Peru, as probably everywhere, the reproductive hierarchy dramatically paralleled the social hierarchy. Petty chiefs were by law allowed up to seven women; governors of a hundred were given eight women; leaders of a thousand got 15 women; chiefs over a million got 30 women. Kings had access to temples filled with women; no lord had less than 700 at his disposal. Typically, the "poor Indian" took whatever was left. Very generally, the youngest, often prepubescent, most virginal, and prettiest girls were selected from among those throughout a kingdom to serve their king; they were kept strictly cloistered against the possibility of infidelity; and kings might possibly, again, have increased their production of grandchildren by favoring polygynous sons (see Dickemann, 1979a).

These results, too, are somewhat at odds with alternative theories. Economic theories suggest that men choose to take more than one wife either because women are themselves net economic assets, or because the children they produce are. Either of these conditions would, of course, make it cheaper for a man to collect a harem. But, neither explains why men should be concerned with the fidelity of their wives, often preferring prepubescent virgins and subjecting them to strict claustration. In fact, if the end of marriage is the production of eco-nomically helpful children, assistance on the part of other men in their production, especially in a huge harem which one man might find it difficult to service alone, should be actively sought out. If the end of marriage is the acquisition of economically helpful women, the selec-tion of 8-year-old virgins and their claustration might both in some ways minimize their productive contribution. The theory that polygyny serves a political function, by creating ties of blood, relies ultimately

upon a biological explanation, kin selection; and the theory that polygyny serves a prestige function can easily be turned on its head: men
are likely to associate prestige with things to which they *a priori* aspire.

These conclusions may most concisely be summarized statistically.
Again, the number of levels in jurisdictional hierarchies has already
been coded by Murdock and Provost (1973) for standard sample societies. To these figures were added a dichotomous coding for the presence or absence of despotism, and a four-level categorization for the
number of women kept simultaneously in the leader's harem, both for
the present sample of 104 politically autonomous groups. Last, a dichotomous code was added on the amount of perquisites leaders took
in arbitration, either greater than or less than equal to bride price or a
bride each time. In Appendix II, each of these variables is explicitly
defined.

All of the coded data for each of the 104 societies in the sample are
listed in Table 5.1. Periods indicate missing data, a consequence of
ethnographic information being too vague to make a reasonable deter-
mination, or absent altogether. In the table, societies are identified first
by number in the Murdock and White sample, and then by group or
subgroup name. The next six columns specify, in order, world area,
degree of political autonomy, number of levels in the jurisdictional
hierarchy, presence or absence of despotism, amount of perquisites
received in arbitration, and, finally, size of the ruler's harem.

In order to test the predicted positive relationships among hierarchy,
despotism, perquisites, and polygyny, each of these four variables was
first correlated with every other in the 104-society world sample, and in
two hemispheric subsamples as well. These include an Old World
sample, made up of societies in Africa, the Circum-Mediterranean, and
East Eurasia (totaling 39 groups), and a New World-Pacific sample,
made up of societies in North America, South and Central America, and
the Insular Pacific (65 groups).

Tables 5.2-5.4 present the results of these correlations. Overall, they
offer good preliminary support for each prediction (see Havlicek and
Peterson, 1977). Relationships are less significant between hierarchy
and the other variables; a look at the raw data in Table 5.1 will show
that they are weakest in peasant societies within modern state hierarchies. It is quite interesting to note that under such hierarchies, both the
use of power to effect a biased resolution of conflicts of interest, and
reproductive rewards in the form of large harems, decline.

The strongest exceptions are all from such relatively modern societies. Altogether, eight focal groups in this sample can be characterized
as peasant societies within four-level state hierarchies: Egypt in 1950
(sample society number 43), Turkey in 1950 (number 47), the Punjab

Table 5.1. Cross-Cultural Codes

No.	Name	1	2	3	4	5	6
1	Nama Hottentot	A	U	2	1	1	1
2	Kung Bushmen	A	U	1	1	.	1
4	Lozi	A	U	4	2	1	.
5	Mbundu	A	U	3	1	1	3
6	Suku	A	A	4	1	1	3
7	Bemba	A	U	4	2	1	3
9	Hadza	A	U	0	1	.	1
12	Ganda	A	A	4	2	2	4
13	Mbuti Pygmies	A	U	0	1	.	1
16	Tiv	A	U	2	1	1	2
18	Fon	A	A	4	2	2	4
19	Ashanti	A	U	4	2	2	4
28	Azande	A	U	3	2	2	4
29	Fur	C	A	4	2	1	.
30	Otoro Nuba	A	U	0	1	1	2
33	Kafa	C	A	4	2	2	3
34	Masai	A	U	1	1	1	3
35	Konso	C	U	2	1	1	2
41	Ahaggaren Tuareg	C	A	3	1	1	.
42	Riffians	C	U	3	1	1	1
43	Egyptians	C	A	4	1	1	2
44	Hebrews	C	A	3	1	1	3
45	Babylonians	C	A	4	1	.	.
46	Rwala Bedouin	C	U	2	1	1	1
47	Turks	C	A	4	1	.	1
48	Gheg Albanians	C	U	2	1	1	1
49	Romans	C	A	4	1	1	.
51	Irish	C	A	3	1	.	1
59	West Punjabi	E	A	4	1	.	1
66	Khalka Mongols	E	U	4	1	1	1
67	Lolo	E	U	1	1	.	1
75	Khmer	E	A	4	2	2	4
76	Siamese	E	A	4	1	.	1
77	Semang	E	A	1	1	.	1
79	Andamanese	E	U	1	1	.	1
80	Forest Vedda	E	U	0	1	.	1
81	Menabe Tanala	E	U	2	1	1	2
86	Tawi-Tawi Badjau	I	U	1	1	.	1
90	Tiwi	I	U	0	1	.	3
91	Aranda	I	U	1	1	.	2
94	Kapauku	I	U	2	1	1	1
100	Tikopia	I	U	2	1	1	1
101	Bunlap	I	U	1	1	.	1
102	Mbau Fijians	I	A	3	2	2	4
104	Maori	I	A	2	1	.	2
105	Marquesans	I	A	2	1	.	2
106	Samoans	I	A	3	2	2	3
107	Makin Gilbertese	I	A	2	1	1	3
111	Palauans	I	A	3	1	.	3
114	Chekiang Chinese	E	A	4	1	.	1
116	Koreans	E	A	4	1	.	1
122	Ingalik	N	U	1	1	.	2

Table 5.1 *continued*

123	Aleut	N	U	2	1	.	2
124	Copper Eskimo	N	U	0	1	.	1
125	Montagnais	N	U	1	1	.	2
126	Micmac	N	U	1	1	.	2
127	Northern Saulteaux	N	U	1	1	.	2
128	Slave	N	U	1	1	.	1
129	Kaska	N	U	1	1	.	1
130	Eyak	N	U	1	1	.	1
131	Masset Haida	N	U	1	1	.	3
132	Bellacoola	N	U	1	1	.	2
133	Twana	N	U	1	1	.	1
134	Yurok	N	U	0	1	.	2
135	Eastern Pomo	N	U	1	1	.	1
136	Lake Yokuts	N	U	1	1	1	1
137	Wadadika Paiute	N	U	1	1	.	2
138	Klamath	N	U	1	1	.	2
139	Lower Kutenai	N	U	1	1	.	2
140	Gros Ventre	N	U	2	1	.	2
141	Hidatsa	N	A	1	1	.	2
142	Skidi Pawnee	N	U	2	1	.	2
143	Omaha	N	U	2	1	.	1
144	Huron	N	U	3	1	1	1
145	Upper Creek	N	U	3	1	.	2
146	Natchez	N	U	3	2	.	3
147	Comanche	N	U	1	1	.	2
148	Chiricahua Apache	N	U	2	1	.	2
149	Zuni	N	U	1	1	.	1
150	Havasupai	N	U	1	1	.	1
151	Papago	N	U	1	1	.	2
153	Aztec	N	A	3	2	2	4
157	Bribri Talamanca	S	U	1	1	.	2
158	Cuna	S	A	2	1	.	2
159	Goajiro	S	U	2	1	.	2
160	Haitians	S	A	4	1	.	2
161	Callinago	S	U	1	1	.	2
162	Warrau	S	U	1	1	.	2
163	Yanomamo	S	U	1	1	.	2
165	Saramacca	S	U	3	1	1	1
169	Jivaro	S	U	0	1	.	2
170	Amahuaca	S	U	0	1	.	2
171	Inca	S	A	4	2	.	4
173	Siriono	S	U	1	1	.	2
174	Nambicuara	S	U	1	1	.	2
175	Trumai	S	U	1	1	.	1
177	Tupinamba	S	U	2	1	.	3
178	Botocudo	S	U	1	1	.	1
179	Shavante	S	U	1	1	.	1
181	Cayua	S	U	1	1	.	1
182	Lengua	S	U	1	1	.	1
183	Abipon	S	U	1	1	.	2
185	Tehuelche	S	U	1	1	.	2
186	Yaghan	S	U	1	1	.	1

Table 5.2. World Correlation Matrix

	Hierarchy	Despotism	Polygyny
Despotism	.5221** (n = 104)		
Polygyny	.3800** (n = 99)	.7185** (n = 99)	
Perquisites	.3845* (n = 34)	.8124** (n = 34)	.7697** (n = 30)

*p<.05.
**p<.01.

also in 1950 (number 59), Mongolia in 1920 (number 66), China in 1936 (number 114), Thailand in 1955 (number 76), Korea in 1947 (number 116), and Haiti in 1935 (number 160). In the literature on each, conflict resolution is discussed in authoritative accounts only at the local level. Even at the national level, although in many cases the contemporary situation may be difficult to ascertain, conflict resolution in groups possessing the capability of employing modern technology appears generally to be less biased. Historically, especially preindustrially, the governments of some of these groups were notoriously despotic. However, in the focal period described none of them was. In a sample restricted to fully fleshed out accounts of preindustrial groups, correlations between hierarchy and despotism, perquisites, and polygyny, even more closely approach unity.

It is important that the predicted relationships hold up across world areas. Table 5.5 shows results of student's t tests for associations between despotism and both hierarchy and polygyny in each of three

Table 5.3. Old World Correlation Matrix

	Hierarchy	Despotism	Polygyny
Despotism	.4452** (n = 39)		
Polygyny	.3995* (n = 34)	.7947** (n = 34)	
Perquisites	.4006* (n = 25)	.7493** (n = 25)	.7555** (n = 21)

*p<.05.
**p<.01.

Table 5.4 New World Correlation Matrix

	Hierarchy	Despotism	Polygyny
Despotism	.5498** ($n=65$)		
Polygyny	.3977** ($n=65$)	.6417** ($n=65$)	
Perquisites	.5735 ($n=9$)	1.0000** ($n=9$)	.8552** ($n=9$)

*$p<.05$.
**$p<.01$.

Table 5.5 Student's *t* Values for Hierarchy and Polygyny by Despotism, for Three Major Subsamples

	Hierarchy	Polygyny
World sample (104 societies)		
Africa/ *Circum-Mediterranean*	$t=3.038$ ($n=28$) $p=.0054$	$t=5.276$ ($n=23$) $p<.0001$
East Eurasia/ *Insular Pacific*	$t=1.592$ ($n=23$) $p=.1264$	$t=4.814$ ($n=23$) $p<.0001$
North America/ *South and Central America*	$t=4.526$ ($n=53$) $p<.0001$	$t=6.053$ ($n=53$) $p<.0001$
Preindustrial sample (96 societies)		
Africa/ *Circum-Mediterranean*	$t=3.516$ ($n=26$) $p=.0018$	$t=4.981$ ($n=21$) $p=.0001$
East Eurasia/ *Insular Pacific*	$t=3.816$ ($n=18$) $p=.0015$	$t=4.079$ ($n=18$) $p=.0009$
North America/ *South and Central America*	$t=5.322$ ($n=52$) $p<.0001$	$t=6.030$ ($n=52$) $p<.0001$

major world regions (see Havlicek and Peterson, 1974). It has been argued that the best test against the possibility that results are due to historical diffusion, or network autocorrelation, as Galton's problem has been reinterpreted, is a demonstration that predicted associations replicate across subsamples (White, Burton, and Dow, 1981; Dow,

Burton, and White, 1982; Dow, 1984; Dow, Burton, White, and Reitz, 1984; Dow, White, and Burton, 1984; Dow, 1985). The results are, again, consistently strong, particularly in samples made up exclusively of preindustrial societies.

Finally, the predicted cause and effect relationship among these variables has been tested using regression equations. Pending publication of a standard sample network autocorrelation program (Burton and White, 1985; Reitz, Dow, Burton, and White, 1985), the best solution to Galton's problem is, again, a demonstration that results replicate across world regions. In this case, dummy variables were used to assign each society to one of the six world areas, and used to control for regional effects. Results of these tests are presented in Table 5.6.

They, again, strongly support the prediction that hierarchical positions of strength afford proportionate exploitation in conflict resolution (despotism), which in turn affords proportionate access to the means to

Table 5.6 World Sample Regressions

Variable	Coefficient	p
Hierarchy → polygyny ($R^2 = .3166$)		
Constant	1.3057	.0800
Hierarchy	.3637	.0001
Africa	.4344	.1219
Circum-Mediterranean	−.7301	.0314
East Eurasia	−.9009	.0041
Insular Pacific	.1109	.6993
North America	−.0243	.9128
Despotism → polygyny ($R^2 = .5592$)		
Constant	−.2255	.3788
Despotism	1.9548	.0001
Africa	.1440	.5274
Circum-Mediterranean	−.2799	.2700
East Eurasia	−.5434	.0231
Insular Pacific	.0282	.9026
North America	−.0812	.6481
Hierarchy, despotism → polygyny ($R^2 = .5681$)		
Constant	−.1702	.5092
Hierarchy	.0940	.1749
Despotism	1.7752	.0001
Africa	.1175	.6055
Circum-Mediterranean	−.4177	.1260
East Eurasia	−.6506	.0099
Insular Pacific	.0101	.9650
North America	−.0727	.6817

reproduction (polygyny). As indicated in this table, the effects of hierarchy upon polygyny are indirect, via effects on despotism as an intermediary variable. This is consistent with the prediction. It should also be pointed out that hierarchy probably serves here as a fair proxy for group size, a demographic constraint in some cases on the number of women collectable in a harem (Betzig, 1982).

Overall, these conclusions are starkly in line with the Darwinian hypothesis that individuals will exploit positions of strength in resolving conflicts in their own interest, and that ultimately they will seek reproductive rewards. These statistical results confirm the impression left by the much more compelling ethnographic facts.

An outstanding problem remains, however, unsolved: Why does the prediction fail to hold up in modern groups? A decline in both despotism and differential reproduction seems to coincide with industrialization. The last chapter suggests what might, at least in part, account for that trend.

> When all conditions are unequal, no inequality is so great as to offend the eye, whereas the slightest dissimilarity is odious in the midst of general uniformity; the more complete this uniformity is, the more insupportable the sight of such a difference becomes. Hence it is natural that the love of equality should constantly increase together with equality itself, and that it should grow by what it feeds on.
> —Alexis de Tocqueville (1840 [1945]:312)

6

DEMOCRACY

On June 17, 1972, five men were arrested in a burglary attempt at the headquarters of the Democratic National Committee in the Watergate complex in Washington, D. C. The break in was incremental to a "basic strategy" of political spying, involving burglaries and wiretapping, and sabotage, under the wholesome rubric of "ratfucking," including following members of opposition party families, assembling dossiers on their personal lives, and attempting to disrupt their campaigns. Over the course of more than a year, these activities were gradually uncovered. So was the attempt to cover up, involving destruction of evidence, bribery, and possible blackmail against attempts to break ranks. Members and readers of the American press were shocked (Bernstein and Woodward, 1975). Almost two years after his overwhelmingly popular election, the president of the United States resigned.

Allegations as to the pleasure leaders have taken in women withstanding, and the power of kinship and cash to bias an arbiter obtaining, the contrast between the divine rights of kings and relative lack of privilege under contemporary American presidents is stark. It would appear that, under recent conditions, despotism and differential reproduction have begun to level off in tandem.

That individuals in preindustrial groups exploit hierarchical positions of strength to bias the resolution of conflicts in their interest, and to take proportionate reproductive rewards, has by now been made abundantly clear. These conclusions are consistent with the Darwinian theory that individuals have evolved to strive to maximize their genetic representation in descendent generations by the production of children, grandchildren, and other close kinsmen. Under what conditions such inequities initially arose, and are now apparently declining, remain important questions. A tentative attempt will be made in conclusion to speculate as to what these conditions were and are.

CONDITIONS PAST

N. A. Boulanger, one of the many eighteenth century writers on despotism, eliminated the possibility that despotic authority might have extended itself by force. "For, by what means, with what arms, can a man be subjected, who enjoys the liberty of running away . . . ?" (1764:5). In the simplest societies, fission is an option to continued struggle or subordination.

Irreconcilable differences in central African Mbuti bands led eventually to a physical break (Turnbull, 1965). As Lee and De Vore (1968:9) later generalized, fission commonly follows conflict in hunting and gathering groups. Lee subsequently elaborated on the process among the Kalahari !Kung, arguing, "the major disadvantage of social life in larger groups is the increased frequency of conflict" (1979:366). Disputes were most frequent and intense where the greatest numbers were gathered together. An increased concentration of population necessitated foraging across a wider radius; people did not always give their fair share; conflicts which were a fact of life in groups of any size amplified as they grew in size. The result: "People get on each other's nerves. . . . Hunters say 'to hell with it.' . . . Foragers have a great deal of latitude to vote with their feet" (p. 367).

The Tanzanian Hadza, like the !Kung, had no institutionalized authority, nor even a sense of corporate identity. Woodburn (1968) referred to Hadza groups simply as "camps": members neither united to perform any common activity, nor acknowledged a bond in opposition to other groups. According to Woodburn, "Individuals and groups move from place to place far more frequently than is strictly necessary if movement is seen simply as a means of providing the best possible access to supplies of food and water;" people moved to satisfy the "slightest whim" (p. 106). It was, again, in large part the "divisive effects of quarrels" which kept the camps small.

Similarly, Madagascar Menabe (Linton, 1933:148), Brazilian Shavante (Maybury-Lewis, 1967), Venezuelan Yanomamo (Chagnon, 1974, 1983), and other factions defeated or likely to be defeated in a conflict of interest fissioned; when they did, individuals took along their closest kinsmen (e.g., Chagnon, 1975, 1979b, 1981; cf. Hurd, 1983). "The natural bias is to independence and rather insubordinate ideas. . . . Cuastro's dying words, 'I die as I have lived—no caique orders me,' aptly express the prevailing feeling on this subject" in southern South American Tehuelche society, and generally (Musters, 1873:193-194). Even where authority is tolerated to some degree, in the words of Levi-Strauss, "If the authority of the chief becomes too demanding, if he monopolizes too great a number of women, if he is not capable in periods of need of resolving food problems, discontent is created, individuals or families break away" (1948:101). "Simple" societies have probably always been "fissioning" societies.

On the other hand, avoidance has not always been an option. Gouldsbury and Sharpe (1911:22), for example, wrote of Bemba despotism:

> It seems truly astonishing that the Awemba themselves, to say nothing of the other conquered tribes, endured such a rigorous administration. But though the writer asked Zapair, and, later, some of the older men of the common people, why they remained passive when they could easily have escaped, the reply was, "Where could we flee to? If we reached the village of a foreign tribe, such as the Washinga, they would say, 'Here are the Awemba, with the *mtoso* neck-mark!' and fall upon us, and slay us! A Shinga or Winamwanga chief would fear to harbour us, and, if they did not kill us in revenge, would simply send us back under escort to Chitimukulu."

Where groups have grown complex, avenues to fission may have been, literally, closed. Such societies have been, to a greater or lesser extent, "circumscribed" (see Carneiro, 1970).

Individuals may adaptively tolerate increasing inequity for two reasons: they must receive a compensating benefit, or avoid a greater cost. The cost of tolerating overlordship may in part be offset by benefits of group membership, such as increased opportunities for reciprocity (e.g., Sahlins, 1958). In addition, as Spencer, in 1876, noted, "the structure of the habitat, as facilitating or impeding communication, and as rendering escape easy or hard, has much to do with the size of the aggregate formed" [(1967):74].

Robert Carneiro, in 1970, argued that state evolution was most likely to occur where groups defeated in war were prevented from fleeing from subjugation. He outlined three forms of circumscription. First, geographic obstacles, such as the Andes, or, second, the cost of leaving an area rich in resources, such as Mesopotamia, for areas of relative deprivation, might serve to pen in a population. Each of these might effectively serve to increase population pressure (see Harner, 1968; Sanders and Price, 1968). Third, population pressure itself, or being surrounded by often hostile groups, might serve to make a people "socially circumscribed" (Chagnon, 1968a). Villages at the center of Yanomamo occupied territory in Venezuela, for example, are larger, conduct more heated warfare, and have more powerful leaders than those on the fringe (Chagnon, 1968b, 1974, 1983).

At the same time, the advantages of integration may offset the costs to the majority of individuals of increasing exploitation. Again, as Sahlins (1958) and others (e.g., Wittfogel, 1957) have recently stressed, group expansion and hierarchy formation may be explained in part as a response to the demand for an organizing function, such as irrigation or redistribution. As many theorists have stressed, another essential advantage to central organization may be its role in determining a society's success in war (e.g., Spencer, 1876; Service, 1962, 1975; Bigelow, 1971; Alexander, 1971, 1974, 1979; Strate, 1982).

As William Irons (1979b) has pointed out, "circumscription" may most broadly be defined as the net benefit, or relatively lower cost, of remaining in a group for any individual member. These benefits and costs may be multiply determined (e.g., Flannery, 1972), including both geological and social resources, and both geological and social obstacles. Factors relevant to an individual's decision, ultimately motivated toward reproduction, may constitute constraints increasing population pressure, or ratios of "circumscription," effecting increased sedentarization and subsistence intensification (Boserup, 1965), in addition to the potential for increasing social organization (Betzig, 1982; cf. Vehrencamp, 1983).

But a concentration of people does not, in itself, constitute a polity. Given an aggregate of individuals drawn together by the net benefit to each of remaining in an area, that is, within a "circumscribing" context, the use of force in the resolution of conflicts of interest may to a substantial extent politically define societies. In any such aggregate, force may be manifested along two dimensions. It may be symmetrically distributed, along a horizontal axis; or it may be asymmetrically concentrated, along a vertical line. In the very broadest sense, the asymmetrical and symmetrical use of force may be conceived of respectively as "law," or the privileged use of force by one party over another, and "war," or a relative balance of power.

All antagonistic interaction can be conceived of along one of these dimensions (cf. Bohannan, 1967b:xiii). Within a family, for example, a father may "lay down the law;" similarly, imperialist powers may extend the long arm of colonial law over relatively powerless groups. On the other hand, rivals in roughly equal positions of strength may wage "war" against one another; and when social factions are unable to dominate each other, the result may be feud or "civil war" (cf. Hoebel, 1954:330).

The definition of social boundaries by the "legal" use of force within and "war" among more equal forces without is not without precedent in ethnographic accounts. Nadel, for example, wrote of the Nubian hills Otoro that in the end both the internal and external identity of a polity must be described in terms of force. "The external collective identity fulfills itself in the concerted action of war or similar forms of aggression . . . ; and the internal identity means essentially the maintenance of peace, the acceptance of a common system of law and order. . . . The basic facts of political existence will always remain visible in the sharp differentiation between the use of force within and without the group" (1947:146; cf., e.g., Evans Pritchard, 1940). Within a circumscribing context, the way in which conflicts of interest are resolved may thus delineate political groups.

Within a polity, hierarchy, like "law," may be, and has been, understood in part as a result of the asymmetrical resolution of conflicts of interest (e.g., Engels, 1884; Fried, 1967; Terray, 1972). It may also be, and has been, understood as an institution arising in the common interest (e.g., Spencer, 1876; Wittfogel, 1957; Sahlins, 1958). To what extent these "conflict" and "integration" pressures gave rise to hierarchies must remain a subject of speculation (Service, 1978).

The most straightforward Darwinian prediction must be that power will be exploited to the extent that "circumscription," broadly defined, goes up; that is, to the extent that subjects have no option but to put up with the arrangement. As much as they are able to resolve conflicts in their own interest, then, men in power should have evolved to seek out reproductive rewards. The evidence, again, strongly suggests that they have done just that.

CONDITIONS PRESENT

At some point in social evolution, however, a watershed is crossed; both despotism and differential reproduction apparently fall off as hierarchical organization continues to grow more complex. Only one condition favors the adaptive sacrifice of an immediate reproductive advantage at any level of selection, and that is one which yields a long-term reproductive gain.

In part, such a beneficial sacrifice might be made through simple reciprocity (e.g., Trivers, 1971). The ability of a subordinate to aid a powerful man is an ability that can be bargained for, with net reproductive benefits to both. Perhaps a more interesting possibility is a more indirect form of reciprocity, by which a subject might gain favor by contributing to the welfare of a man in power by abetting the welfare of the group. In this connection, the "parliament of genes" analogy (Leigh, 1971, 1977; cf. Hardin, 1968), in which units of heredity are supposed to enforce cooperation within the genome in order to reap a net reproductive reward in individual competition, may be an appropriate one (Alexander and Borgia, 1978). To the extent that their subjects' cooperation is necessary to yield them individual reproductive advantage in intergroup competition, individuals in positions of power may find it to be in their own interests to share the "spoils of war." Alexander, in 1975, suggested that successful polygynists may have conceded to trim the size of their harems in order to increase the probability of their survival and reproduction in intergroup competition. The apparently concurrent approach toward equality under the law might be similarly understood (Alexander, 1978).

Durkheim (1893), adopting Spencer's (1876) analogy of society as an organism, contrasted the "organic" integration of complex societies by the interworkings of their parts with what he called "mechanical" solidarity, or the attraction of like to like in simple groups. If the arguments above are right, then in a homogeneous, mechanically integrated group, every individual may, as far as another with conflicts of interest is concerned, be easily replaced. However, as organic solidarity arises, the ability of any member of society to perform a specialized function may enable him or her to demand concessions from individuals in power. This should be so to the extent that their efforts aid in their benefactor's reproduction, either directly, or indirectly by adding to the reproductive assets at the disposal of the group.

Bargaining power is likely to go up if individuals' skills are sought by a number of competing groups. Mercenaries, for example, from the first have been able to obtain productive and reproductive privileges in return for the part they played in war. Most recently, the defection of, for example, scientists may be understood in a similar way; people in power have been forced to make concessions for what they have to offer, either in particular cases or as a matter of policy, in order to attract them.

Again, by wearing the marks of their trade, special subjects in Ganda were exempt from despotic acts (Kagwa, 1934:81). Even in the simplest groups, reproductive rewards are frequently conceded to young men for military success. In, among others, Comanche society, "If someone distinguishes himself in bravery and in actions made against his enemies, or something of a similar nature, some fathers give them even of their daughters" (Cabello y Robles, 1961:178). In more circumscribed groups, these privileges persist. Natchez stinkards were able to earn the status of honored men with an enemy scalp (Swanton, 1911:104); success in obtaining captives was integral to an Aztec's attainment of privilege and status (e.g., Sahagun, 1951b:76-77). And under the Empire, Roman soldiers and veterans, like equestrians, decurions, and senators, were privileged before the law (Garnsey, 1968, 1970). This trend, of course, continued in the relationship of lords to vassals in the Middle Ages, as the latter were increasingly rewarded with wealth, land, and the right to bequeath their assets to heirs in return for their valor in war (e.g., Cantor, 1969:217-219).

Eventually, as European society over the past few centuries has been becoming an "organism" (Spencer, 1876; Durkheim, 1893), so has it tended toward democratization. As industrialization has given rise to specialization, it may also have brought on reproductive concessions. In ensuring an advantage in intergroup competition, inventors may, again, early have become as important as successful warriors. Concessions by hierarchy heads in positions to make them, in power, legal privilege, productive resources, and women, may have to have been proportionate in order to enlist their cooperation. Insofar as the increasing sophistication of their training made them irreplaceable, tradesmen, and eventually technicians, may have to have been rewarded as well. In the long run, where intergroup competition became most important, and success depended upon a sufficient number of specialized occupations, concessions might have been made to members of an increasing number of essential social "organs." The achievements of the labor movement might to a substantial extent depend upon the importance of workers to a society's efforts toward collective defense, as well as on their more direct ability to contribute to the productive and reproductive efforts of men in power.

In general, bargaining power should of course increase with scarcity in the number of people qualified to fill any position. Even the least skilled laborers might become more valuable as their numbers decline, and/or as need for their services goes up, although immigration may often afford an alternative to men in power. As markets have expanded with industrialization, the scarcity, and so the value, of labor may have increased as well.

Although specialization in a number of modern states is increasing with industrialization, not all appear to have made parallel developments toward democratization. Although the invention and manufacture of such a technology may be likely to necessitate leveling incentives, the adoption of such innovations ready made by intelligence or trade may not require concessions quite as great. As Elman Service, in an inspired essay, "The Law of Evolutionary Potential" (1960), suggested, in Third-world countries lacking the material edge brought on in large part by a history of successful war with other groups, capital sufficient to obtain a competitive military technology may have to be extracted from a subsistence-oriented peasantry. "The extraction of capital must be forced," and thus, might take on a despotic aspect (pp. 115-116).

This problem is clearly an open niche for research. The essential questions following from the argument are: first, how closely, and according to what rough time schedule, have despotism, or differential legal privilege, and differential reproduction, especially concubinage, declined?; second, how closely did that decline coincide with the increasing specialization and/or scarcity of labor, and other events making the interests of men in power and their subordinates overlap? They are important problems, but will have to wait on a later solution.

A recent report of the United Nations Human Rights Commission conservatively estimated that, worldwide, at least two million people have been the victims of arbitrary executions in the last fifteen years (*Chicago Tribune*, February 17, 1983). Despotism is hardly yet a historical artifact. It is humbly to be hoped that it may yet become one, and that, to some extent, an understanding of human history as natural history will help.

Appendix I

DESCRIPTION OF THE SAMPLE*

1. **Nama Hottentot**

Sampling Province: 1 (Hottentots)
Ethnographic Atlas Number: Aa3
Language: Khoisan (Southern)
Location: The Gei/Khauan tribe (27° 30'S, 17°E)
Period: Reconstructed for 1860, just prior to their decimation and
    loss of independence in the Herero War
Authorities: Schultze; Schapera (secondary)

2. **Kung Bushmen**

Sampling Province: 2 (Bushmen)
Ethnographic Atlas Number: Aa1
Language: Khoisan (Southern)
Location: The Agau Kung of the Nyae Nyae region (19°50'S, 20°35'E)
Period: 1950, when the Marshalls began their study of this still un-
    acculturated group.
Authority: L. Marshall

4. **Lozi**

Sampling Province: 4 (Sotho)
Ethnographic Atlas Number: Ab3
Language: Niger-Congo (Bantoid)
Location: The ruling Luyana (14° to 18°20'S, 22° to 25°E)
Period: 1900, at the height of Barotse political expansion
Authority: Gluckman

*Adapted from Murdock and White (1969).

5. **Mbundu**

Sampling Province: 5 (Southwestern Bantu)
Ethnographic Atlas Number: Ab5
Language: Niger-Congo (Bantoid)
Location: Bailundo subtribe (12°15′S, 16°30′E)
Period: 1890, just prior to Portuguese conquest and missionization
Authority: Childs

6. **Suku**

Sampling Province: 6 (Western Central Bantu)
Ethnographic Atlas Number: Ac17
Language: Niger-Congo (Bantoid)
Location: Feshi Territory (6°S, 18°E)
Period: 1920, just prior to their loss of independence
Authority: Kopytoff, Torday and Joyce

7. **Bemba**

Sampling Province: 7 (Eastern Central Bantu)
Ethnographic Atlas Number: Ac3
Language: Niger-Congo (Bantoid)
Location: Zambia (9° to 12°S, 29° to 32°E)
Period: 1897, just prior to the advent of British administration
Authority: Richards

9. **Hadza**

Sampling Province: 10 (Rift)
Ethnographic Atlas Number: Aa9
Language: Khoisan (Northern)
Location: The small Hadza tribe as a whole (3°20′ to 4°10′S, 34°40′ to 35°25′E)
Period: 1930, when still unacculturated
Authority: Kohl-Larsen; Woodburn

12. **Ganda**

Sampling Province: 13 (Lacustrine Bantu)
Ethnographic Atlas Number: Ad7
Language: Niger-Congo (Bantoid)
Location: Kyaddondo district (0°20′N, 32°30′E)
Period: 1875, just prior to the founding of Kampala and the initiation
    of significant administrative changes
*Authorities:*Roscoe; Mair

13. **Mbuti Pygmies**

Sampling Province: 15 (Pygmies)
Ethnographic Atlas Number: Aa5
Language: Niger-Congo (Bantoid)
Location: The Epulu net-hunters of the Ituri Forest (1°30′ to 2°N,
    28°15′ to 28°25′E)
Period: 1950, just prior to Turnbull's field work
Authorities: Turnbull; Schebesta

16. **Tiv**

Sampling Province: 29 and 30 (Nigerian Plateau)
Ethnographic Atlas Number: Ah3
Language: Niger-Congo (Bantoid)
Location: Benue Province (6°30′ to 8°N, 8° to 10°E)
Period: 1920, prior to extensive organizational changes by the British
Authorities: Bohannan; East

18. **Fon**

Sampling Province: 19 (Slave Coast)
Ethnographic Atlas Number: Af1
Language: Niger-Congo (Kwa)
Location: The vicinity of Abomey (7°12′N, 1°56′E)
Period: 1890, prior to the conquest of the Dahomean kingdom by the
    French
Authorities: Herskovits; Le Herissé

19. **Ashanti**

Sampling Province: 20 (Akan)
Ethnographic Atlas Number: Af3
Language: Niger-Congo (Kwa)
Location: The state of Kumasi (6° to 8°N, 0° to 3°W)
Period: 1895, just prior to British conquest
Authorities: Rattray; Fortes

28. **Azande**

Sampling Province: 33 and 34 (North Equatoria)
Ethnographic Atlas Number: Ai3
Language: Niger-Congo (Eastern)
Location: Yambio chiefdom (4°20' to 5°50'N, 27°40' to 28°50'E)
Period: 1905, just prior to British conquest and the collapse of the
    Avungara political system
Authority: Evans-Pritchard

29. **Fur**

Sampling Province: 32 (Wadai and Darfur)
Ethnographic Atlas Number: Cb17
Language: Furian
Location: Western Darfur around Jebel Marra (13°30'N, 25°30'E)
Period: 1880, prior to effective Egyptian subjugation
Authorities: Felkin; Beaton

30. **Otoro**

Sampling Province: 35 (Nuba)
Ethnographic Atlas Number: Ai10
Language: Kordofanian
Location: Nuba Hills (11°20'N, 30°40'E)
Period: 1930, prior to substantial migration into the plains
Authority: Nadel

33. **Kafa**

Sampling Province: 39 (Western Cushites)
Ethnographic Atlas Number: Ca30
Language: Afroasiatic (Western Cushitic)
Location: The politically unified Kafa as a whole (6°50′ to 7°45′N,
    35°30′ to 37°E)
Period: 1905, the date of Beiber's field work
Authority: Bieber

34. **Masai**

Sampling Province: 38 (Southern Nilotes)
Ethnographic Atlas Number: Aj2
Language: Chari-Nile (Eastern)
Location: The Kisonko or Southern Masai of Tanzania (1°30′ to
    5°30′S, 35° to 37°30′E)
Period: 1900, about the time of Merker's field work
Authorities: Merker, Jacob

35. **Konso**

Sampling Province: 40 (Galla-Konso)
Ethnographic Atlas Number: Ca1
Language: Afroasiatic (Eastern Cushitic)
Location: Town of Buso (5°15′N, 37°30′E)
Period: 1935, the date of Jense's field work
Authorities: Hallpike; Jensen

41. **Tuareg**

Sampling Province: 46 (Tuareg)
Ethnographic Atlas Number: Cc9
Language: Afroasiatic (Berber)
Location: Ahaggaren Tuareg (21° to 25°N, 4° to 9°E)
Period: 1900, prior to the French military occupation of the Sahara
Authorities: Nicolaisen; Lhote

42. **Riffians**

Sampling Province: 47 and 48 (Berbers of the Maghreb)
Ethnographic Atlas Number: Cd3
Language: Afroasiatic (Berber)
Location: The Riffians as a whole (34°20′ to 35°30′N, 2°30′ to 4°W)
Period: 1926, at the beginning of Coon's field work
Authority: Coon

43. **Egyptians**

Sampling Province: 49 (Arabs of North Africa)
Ethnographic Atlas Number: Cd2
Language: Afroasiatic (Semitic)
Location: Town and environs of Silwa (24°45′N, 33°E)
Period: 1950, the approximate date of Ammar's field work
Authorities: Ammar, Wilber (secondary)

44. **Hebrews**

Sampling Province: 51 (Jews)
Ethnographic Atlas Number: Cj3
Language: Afroasiatic (Semitic)
Location: Kingdom of Judah (30°30′ to 31°55′N, 34°20′ to 35°30′E)
Period: 621 B.C., the date of promulgation of the Deuternomic laws
Authorities: Old Testament; DeVaux (secondary)

45. **Babylonians**

Sampling Province: 53 (Ancient Mesopotamia)
Ethnographic Atlas Number: Cj4
Language: Afroasiatic (Semitic)
Location: City and environs of Babylon (32°35′N, 44°45′E)
Period: 1750 B.C., at the end of the reign of Hammurabi
Authorities: Pritchard (translation of Hammurabi's law code); Saggs
     (secondary)

46. **Rwala**

Sampling Province: 52 (Arabs of Arabia and the Levant)
Ethnographic Atlas Number: Cj2
Language: Afroasiatic (Semitic)
Location: The Rwala Bedouin of south central Syria and northeastern
        Jordan (31° to 35°30′N, 36° to 41°E)
Period: 1913, early in the periods of field work of Musil and Raswan
Authorities: Musil; Raswan

47. **Turks**

Sampling Province: 54 (Turkey)
Ethnographic Atlas Number: Ci5
Language: Altaic (Turkic)
Location: Northern Anatolian plateau (38°40′ to 40°N, 32°40′ to
        35°50′E)
Period: 1950, during the periods of field work of Stirling and Makal
Authorities: Stirling; Makal

48. **Gheg**

Sampling Province: 55 (Balkans)
Ethnographic Atlas Number: Ce1
Language: Indo-European (Albanian)
Location: Mountain Gheg of northern Albania (41°20′ to 42°N, 19°30′
        to 20°31′E)
Period: 1910, just prior to the expulsion of the Turks in the two
        Balkan Wars
Authorities: Coon; Durham

49. **Romans**

Sampling Province: 56 (Greece and Italy)
Ethnographic Atlas Number: Ce3
Language: Indo-European (Italic)
Location: City and environs of Rome (41°50′N, 13°30′E)
Period: 110 A.D., the twelfth year of Trajan's reign at the approximate
        zenith of the imperial period
Authorities: Pliny the Younger; Carcopino (secondary); Friedlander
        (secondary)

51. Irish

Sampling Province: 57 (Northwestern Europeans)
Ethnographic Atlas Number: Cg3
Language: Indo-European (Celtic)
Location: County Clare (52°40′ to 53°10′N, 8°20′ to 10°W)
Period: 1932, at the time of the field work by Arensberg and Kimball
Authorities: Arensberg and Kimball; Cresswell

59. Punjabi

Sampling Province: 64 (Indus Valley)
Ethnographic Atlas Number: Not in EA
Language: Indo-European (Indic)
Location: The western Punjabi of the village of Mohla (32°30′N, 74°E)
Period: 1950, during the period of Eglar's field work
Authority: Eglar

66. Khalka Mongols

Sampling Province: 82 (Mongols)
Ethnographic Atlas Number: Eb3
Language: Altaic (Mongolic)
Location: Narobanchin temple territory (47° to 47°20′N, 95°10′ to 97°E)
Period: 1920, the approximate date of Vreeland's reconstruction
Authority: Vreeland

67. Lolo

Sampling Province: 84 (Southwest China)
Ethnographic Atlas Number: Ed2
Language: Tibeto-Burman (Akha-Lahu-Lisu-Lolo subfamily)
Location: The independent and relatively unacculturated Lolo of the Taliang Shan mountains (26° to 29°N, 103° to 104°E)
Period: 1910, the approximate date of the field work by D'Ollone
Authorities: D'Ollone; Lin

75. **Khmer**

Sampling Province: 95 (Cambodia)
Ethnographic Atlas Number: Ej5
Language: Mon-Khmer (Khmer)
Location: City of Angkor (13°30'N, 103°50'E), the capital of the old
    Khmer kingdom at its height
Period: 1292, the date of the visit and description by Chou
Authorities: Chou Ta-Kuan; Groslier; Aymonier

76. **Siamese**

Sampling Province: 91 (Thai)
Ethnographic Atlas Number: Ej9
Language: Thai-Kadai
Location: The Central Thai village of Bang Chan (14°N, 100°50'E)
Period: About 1955, the midpoint of the Cornell University research
    project
Authorities: Sharp; L. & J. Hanks

77. **Semang**

Sampling Province: 94 (Semang-Sakai)
Ethnographic Atlas Number: Ej3
Language: Mon-Khmer (Semang-Sekai)
Location: The Jahai subtribe (4°30' to 5°30'N, 101° to 101°30'E)
Period: 1925, at the approximate beginning of Schebesta's field work
Authorities: Schebesta; Evans

79. **Andamanese**

Sampling Province: 92 (Andaman Islands)
Ethnographic Atlas Number: Eh1
Language: Andamanese
Location: Aka-Bea tribe of South Andaman (11°45' to 12°N, 93° to
    93°10'E)
Period: 1860, prior to significant acculturation and depopulation
Authorities: Man; Radcliffe-Brown

80. **Vedda**

Sampling Province: 66 (Ceylon)
Ethnographic Atlas Number: Eh4
Language: Indo-European (Indic)
Location: The Danigala group of Forest Vedda (7°30′ to 8°N, 81° to 81°30′E)
Period: 1860, the date of the observations by Bailey made prior to intensive acculturation
Authorities: Seligman and Seligman; Bailey

81. **Tanala**

Sampling Province: 8 (Madagascar)
Ethnographic Atlas Number: Eh3
Language: Malayo-Polynesian (Hesperonesian)
Location: The Menabe subtribe (22°S, 48°E)
Period: 1925, just prior to Linton's field work
Authority: Linton

86. **Badjau**

Sampling Province: 100 (Badjau or Sea Gypsies)
Ethnographic Atlas Number: Ia13
Language: Malayo-Polynesian (Hesperonesian)
Location: The Badjau of southwestern Tawi-Tawi and adjacent islands of the Sulu Archipelago (5°N, 120°E)
Period: 1963, the date of Nimmo's field work
Authority: Nimmo

90. **Tiwi**

Sampling Province: 108 (Tropical Australia)
Ethnographic Atlas Number: Id3
Language: Australian
Location: Bathurst and Melville Islands (11° to 11°45′S, 130° to 132°E)
Period: 1929, the date of Hart's field work
Authorities: Hart and Pilling; Goodale

91. **Aranda**

Sampling Province: 109 (Central and Southern Australia)
Ethnographic Atlas Number: Id1
Language: Australian
Location: The Arunta Mbainda of Alice Springs (23°30' to 25°S, 132°30' to 134°20'E)
Period: 1896, the date of the early field work by Spencer and Gillen
Authorities: Spencer and Gillen; Strehlow

94. **Kapauku**

Sampling Province: 114 (Northwestern New Guinea)
Ethnographic Atlas Number: Ie1
Language: Papuan (distinct family)
Location: The village of Botukebo in the Kamu Valley (c. 4°S, 36°E)
Period: 1955, the date of Pospisil's first field trip
Authority: Pospisil

100. **Tikopia**

Sampling Province: 124 (Polynesian Outliers)
Ethnographic Atlas Number: Ii2
Language: Malayo-Polynesian (Polynesian)
Location: Tikopia island as a whole (12°30'S, 168°30'E)
Period: 1930, at the conclusion of Firth's first field trip
Authority: Firth

101. **Pentecost**

Sampling Province: 125 and 126 (New Hebrides and Banks Islands)
Ethnographic Atlas Number: Ih3
Language: Malayo-Polnesian (Melanesian)
Location: The village of Bunlap and neighboring intermarrying pagan villages in southeastern Pentecost Island
Period: 1953, the date of the first field trip by the Lanes
Authorities: Lane and Lane

102. **Mbau Fijians**

Sampling Province: 128 (Fiji and Rotuma)
Ethnographic Atlas Number: Not in EA
Language: Malayo-Polynesian (Melanesian)
Location: The island of Mbau off the east coast of Viti Levu (18°S, 178°35'E)
Period: 1840, the approximate date of the best early descriptions
Authorities: Toganivalu; Waterhouse

104. **Maori**

Sampling Province: 130 (Southern Polynesia)
Ethnographic Atlas Number: Ij2
Language: Malayo-Polynesian (Polynesian)
Location: The Nga Puhi tribe of the northern isthmus (35°10' to 35°30'S, 174° to 174°20'E)
Period: 1820, prior to European settlement and missionization
Authorities: Earle; Clarke

105. **Marquesans**

Sampling Province: 131 (Eastern Polynesia)
Ethnographic Atlas Number: Ij3
Language: Malayo-Polynesian (Polynesian)
Location: The Te-i'i chiefdom of southwestern Nuku Hiva Island (8°55'S, 140°10'W)
Period: 1800, at about the time of the earliest reliable descriptions
Authorities: Fleurieu; Forster; Langsdorff

106. **Samoans**

Sampling Province: 129 (Western Polynesia)
Ethnographic Atlas Number: Ii1
Language: Malayo-Polynesian (Polynesian)
Location: The kingdom of Aana in western Upolu Island (13°48' to 14°S, 171°45' to 172°3'W)
Period: 1829, prior to the military defeat of Aana and the beginning of intensive European contact
Authorities: Turner; Stair

107. **Gilbertese**

Sampling Province: 119 (Gilbert Islands)
Ethnographic Atlas Number: If14
Language: Malayo-Polynesian (Carolinian)
Location: The northern Gilbertese of Makin and Butiritari Islands
    (3°30′N, 172°20′E)
Period: Reconstructed for about 1890
Authority: Lambert

111. **Palauans**

Sampling Province: 115 (Palau and Marianas)
Ethnographic Atlas Number: If1
Language: Malayo-Polynesian (Hesperonesian)
Location: The village of Ulimang in northern Babelthuap Island
    (7°30′N, 134°35′E)
Period: 1947, the date of Barnett's field work
Authorities: Barnett; Kramer

114. **Chinese**

Sampling Province: 83 (Chinese)
Ethnographic Atlas Number: Not in EA
Language: Sinitic (Wu Dialect)
Location: The village of Kaihsienkung in northern Chekiang (31°N,
    120°5′E)
Period: 1936, the date of Fei's field work
Authority: Fei

116. **Koreans**

Sampling Province: 80 (Korea)
Ethnographic Atlas Number: Ed1
Language: Korean
Location: The village of Sondup'o and town of Samku Li on Kanghwa
    Island (37°37′N, 126°25′E)
Period: 1947, the date of Osgood's field work
Authority: Osgood

122. **Ingalik**

Sampling Province: 135 (Yukon)
Ethnographic Atlas Number: Na8
Language: Athapaskan (Northern)
Location: The village of Shageluk (62°30′N, 159°30′W)
Period: Reconstructed for 1885, just prior to missionization
Authority: Osgood

123. **Aleut**

Sampling Province: 132 (Western Eskimo)
Ethnographic Atlas Number: Na9
Language: Eskimuan (Aleut)
Location: The Unalaska branch of the Aleut (53° to 57°30′N, 158° to 170°W)
Period: About 1800, prior to intensive acculturation
Authorities: Veniaminov; Sarytschew

124. **Copper Eskimo**

Sampling Province: 133 (Central and Eastern Eskimo)
Ethnographic Atlas Number: Na3
Language: Eskimaun (Eskimo)
Location: The Arctic mainland (66°40′ to 69°20′N, 108° to 117°W)
Period: 1915, during the period of field work by Jenness
Authorities: Jenness; Rasmussen

125. **Montagnais**

Sampling Province: 151 (Cree-Montagnais)
Ethnographic Atlas Number: Na32
Language: Algonkian
Location: The Lake St. John and Mistassini bands (48° to 52°N, 73° to 75°W)
Period: 1910, near the beginning of Speck's field work
Authorities: Speck; Lips

126. **Micmac**

Sampling Province: 152 (Maritime Algonkians)
Ethnographic Atlas Number: Na41
Language: Algonkian
Location: The mainland (43°30′ to 50°N, 60° to 66°W)
Period: 1650, midway in the governorship of Denys
Authorities: Denys; Le Clercq

127. **Saulteaux**

Sampling Province: 153 (Ojibwa)
Ethnographic Atlas Number: Na33
Language: Algonkian
Location: The Northern Saulteaux of the Berens River band (52°N,
    95°30′W)
Period: 1930, at the beginning of Hallowell's field work
Authority: Hallowell

128. **Slave**

Sampling Province: 134 (Northeastern Athapaskans)
Ethnographic Atlas Number: Na17
Language: Athapaskan (Northern)
Location: The vicinity of Fort Simpson (62°N, 122°W)
Period: 1940, just prior to the heavy acculturation following World
    War II
Authorities: Helm (MacNeish); Honigman

129. **Kaska**

Sampling Province: 138 (Carrier-Nahani)
Ethnographic Atlas Number: Na4
Language: Athapaskan (Northern)
Location: The Upper Liard River (60°N, 131°W)
Period: 1900, just prior to intensive missionization
Authority: Honigmann

130. **Eyak**

Sampling Province: 136 (South Central Alaska)
Ethnographic Atlas Number: Nb5
Language: Eyak
Location: The small Eyak tribe as a whole (60° to 61°N, 144° to 146°W)
Period: 1890, prior to full acculturation
Authorities: Birket-Smith and De Laguna

131. **Haida**

Sampling Province: 137 (Northern Northwest Coast)
Ethnographic Atlas Number: Nb1
Language: Skittagetan
Location: The village of Masset (54°N, 132°30'W)
Period: Reconstructed for 1875, immediately prior to missionization
Authorities: Swanton; Murdock

132. **Bellacoola**

Sampling Province: 139 (Wakashan-Bellacoola)
Ethnographic Atlas Number: Nb9
Language: Salishan
Location: The central Bellacoola along the lower Bella Coola River (52°20'N, 126° to 127°W)
Period: 1880, shortly prior to the early field work of Boas
Authorities: McIlwraith; Boas

133. **Twana**

Sampling Province: 140 (Coast Salish)
Ethnographic Atlas Number: Nb2
Language: Salishan
Location: The small Twana tribe as a whole (47°20' to 47°30'N, 123°10' to 123°20'W)
Period: Reconstructed for 1860, prior to missionization
Authorities: Elmendorf; Eells

134. **Yurok**

Sampling Province: 141 (Central Pacific Coast)
Ethnographic Atlas Number: Nb4
Language: Ritwan
Location: The village of Tsurai (41°30′N, 124°W)
Period: 1850, the date of the arrival of Loeffelholtz, the earliest
      ethnographer
Authorities: Kroeber; Heizer and Mills

135. **Pomo**

Sampling Province: 143 (Central California)
Ethnographic Atlas Number: Nc18
Language: Hokan (Kulanapan)
Location: The Eastern Pomo of Clear Lake (39°N, 123°W)
Period: 1850, prior to the inrush of European settlers
Authorities: Gifford; Barrett; Loeb

136. **Yokuts**

Sampling Province: 144 (Southern California)
Ethnographic Atlas Number: Nc24
Language: Penutian (Mariposan)
Location: The Lake Yokuts (35°10′N, 119°20′W)
Period: 1850, prior to the influx of settlers following the gold rush
Authority: Gayton

137. **Paiute**

Sampling Province: 146 and 147 (Great Basin)
Ethnographic Atlas Number: Nd22
Language: Shoshonean
Location: The Wadadika or Harney Valley band of Northern Paiute
      (43° to 44°N, 118° to 120°W)
Period: Reconstructed for about 1870, just prior to the establishment
      of a reservation
Authority: B. Whiting

138. **Klamath**

Sampling Province: 142 and 148 (Southern Plateau and Northeast California)
Ethnographic Atlas Number: Nc8
Language: Sahaptin (Lutuamian)
Location: The Klamath tribe as a whole (42° to 43°15'N, 121°20' to 122°20'W)
Period: 1860, prior to intensive acculturation
Authority: Spier; Gatschet

139. **Kutenai**

Sampling Province: 149 (Nothern Plateau)
Ethnographic Atlas Number: Nd7
Language: Kitunahan
Location: The Lower Kutenai (48°40' to 49°10'N, 116°40'W)
Period: 1890, the date of Chamberlain's field work
Authorities: Turney-High; Chamberlain

140. **Gros Ventre**

Sampling Province: 150 (Northern Plains)
Ethnographic Atlas Number: Ne1
Language: Algonkian
Location: The homogeneous Gros Ventre as a whole (47° to 49°N, 106° to 110°W)
Period: 1880, shortly prior to missionization and the disappearance of the buffalo
Authorities: Flannery; Cooper

141 **Hidatsa**

Sampling Province: 154 (Upper Missouri)
Ethnographic Atlas Number: Ne15
Language: Siouan
Location: The village of Hidatsa (47°N, 101°W)
Period: Reconstructed for 1836, prior to depopulation in a severe smallpox epidemic
Authorities: Bowers; Matthews

142. **Pawnee**

Sampling Province: 159 (Caddoans)
Ethnographic Atlas Number: Nf6
Language: Caddoan
Location: The Skidi or Skiri Pawnee (42°N, 100°W)
Period: Reconstructed for 1867
Authorities: Weltfish; Dorsey and Murie

143. **Omaha**

Sampling Province: 155 (Prairie)
Ethnographic Atlas Number: Nf3
Language: Siouan
Location: The Omaha tribe as a whole (41°10′ to 41°40′N, 96° to 97°W)
Period: 1860, prior to the disappearance of the buffalo
Authorities: Fletcher and La Flesche; Dorsey

144. **Huron**

Sampling Province: 156 (Northeastern Woodlands)
Ethnographic Atlas Number: Ng1
Language: Iroquoian
Location: The Attignawantan (Bear People) and Attigneenongnahac (Cord People) tribes of the Huron Confederacy (44° to 45°N, 78° to 80°W)
Period: 1634, the date of the beginning of Jesuit missionary activity
Authorities: Brébeuf; Sagard-Théodat; Tooker (secondary)

145. **Creek**

Sampling Province: 157 (Southeastern Woodlands)
Ethnographic Atlas Number: Ng3
Language: Natchez-Muskogean (Muskogean)
Location: The Upper Creek of Alabama (32°30′ to 34°20′N, 85°30′ to 86°30′W)
Period: 1800, prior to Tecumseh's rebellion and removal to Oklahoma
Authority: Swanton

146. **Natchez**

Sampling Province: 158 (Lower Mississippi)
Ethnographic Atlas Number: Ng7
Language: Natchez-Muskogean (Natchesan)
Location: The politically integrated Natchez tribe as a whole
(31°30′N, 91°25′W)
Period: 1718, the date of the arrival of the first missionaries and
ethnographers
Authorities: Dumont de Montigny; Le Page du Pratz; Swanton (secondary)

147. **Comanche**

Sampling Province: 160 (Southern Plains)
Ethnographic Atlas Number: Ne3
Language: Shoshonean
Location: The Comanche as a whole (30° to 38°N, 98° to 103°W)
Period: 1870, just prior to pacification and removal to Oklahoma
Authority: Hoebel

148. **Chiricahua Apache**

Sampling Province: 161 (Apache-Tanoan)
Ethnographic Atlas Number: Nh1
Language: Athapaskan (Southern)
Location: The central band or Chiricahua proper (32°N, 109°30′W)
Period: 1870, immediately prior to the reservation period
Authority: Opler

149. **Zuni**

Sampling Province: 162 (Pueblo-Navaho)
Ethnographic Atlas Number: Nh4
Language: Zunian
Location: The village of Zuni (35° to 35°30′N, 108°30′ to 109°W)
Period: 1880, approximately the beginning of the field work of both
Cushing and Stevenson
Authorities: Cushing; Stevenson

150. **Havasupai**

Sampling Province: 145 (Yumans)
Ethnographic Atlas Number: Nd3
Language: Hokan (Yuman)
Location: The small Havasupai tribe as a whole (35°20' to 36°20'N,
111°20' to 113°W)
Period: 1918, at the beginning of Spier's field work
Authority: Spier

151. **Papago**

Sampling Province: 163 (Northwest Mexico)
Ethnographic Atlas Number: Ni2
Language: Piman
Location: The Archie Papago near Sells, Arizona (32°N, 112°W)
Period: 1910, the date of the early observations by Lumholtz
Authorities: Underhill; Lumholtz

153. **Aztec**

Sampling Province: 165 (Central Mexico)
Ethnographic Atlas Number: Nj2
Language: Nahuatlan
Location: The city and environs of Tenochtitlan (19°N, 99°10'W)
Period: 1520, the date of the arrival of the Spaniards
Authorities: Sahagun; Vaillant (secondary)

157. **Bribri**

Sampling Province: 169 (Costa Rica)
Ethnographic Atlas Number: Sa5
Language: Chibchan
Location: The Bribri tribe of the Talamanca nation (9°N, 83°15'W)
Period: 1917, the date of Skinner's field work
Authorities: Stone; Skinner

158. **Cuna**

Sampling Province: 170 (Panama)
Ethnographic Atlas Number: Sa1
Language: Chibchan
Location: The San Blas Archipelago (9° to 9°30′N, 78° to 79°W)
Period: 1927, the date of Nordenskiold's field work
Authorities: Nordenskiold; Wafer; Stout

159. **Goajiro**

Sampling Province: 172 (Northern Colombia and Venezuela)
Ethnographic Atlas Number: Sb6
Language: Arawakan
Location: The homogeneous Goajiro tribe as a whole (11°30′ to
    12°20′N, 71° to 72°30′W)
Period: 1947, the date of the field work by Gutierrez de Pineda
Authorities: Guttierez de Pineda; Bolinder

160. **Haitians**

Sampling Province: 174 (Caribbean Negroes)
Ethnographic Atlas Number: Sb9
Language: Indo-European (Romance)
Location: Mirebalais (18°50′N, 72°10′W)
Period: 1935, the date of the field work by Herskovits
Authorities: Herskovits; Métraux

161. **Callinago**

Sampling Province: 173 (Antillean Indigenes)
Ethnographic Atlas Number: Sb1
Language: Cariban
Location: The island of Dominica (15°30′N, 60°30′W)
Period: Reconstructed for 1650, shortly prior to missionization
Authorities: Breton; Taylor

162. **Warrau**

Sampling Province: 175 and 176 (Orinoco)
Ethnographic Atlas Number: Sc1
Language: Warrauan
Location: The Orinoco delta (8°30′ to 9°50′N, 60°40′ to 62°30′W)
Period: 1935, early in the period of missionary field work by Turrado
    Moreno
Authorities: Turrado Moreno; Wilbert

163. **Yanomamo**

Sampling Province: 177 (Southern Venezuela)
Ethnographic Atlas Number: Not in EA
Language: Yanomaman
Location: The Shamatari subtribe around the village of Bisaasi-teri
    (2° to 2°45′N, 64°30′ to 65°30′W)
Period: 1965, at the time of Chagnon's field work
Authority: Chagnon

165. **Saramacca**

Sampling Province: 179 (Bush Negroes)
Ethnographic Atlas Number: Sc6
Language: Indo-European (Creolized Romance)
Location: The Saramacca group of Bush Negroes in the upper basin of
    the Suriname River (3° to 4°N, 55°30′ to 56°W)
Period: 1928, early in the periods of field work by Herskovits and
    Kahn
Authorities: Kahn; Herskovits

169. **Jivaro**

Sampling Province: 183 (Eastern Ecuador)
Ethnographic Atlas Number: Se3
Language: Jivaran
Location: The Jivaro proper (2° to 4°S, 77° to 79°W)
Period: 1920, near the beginning of Karsten's field work
Authorities: Karsten; Stirling

170. **Amahuaca**

Sampling Province: 184 (Montana)
Ethnographic Atlas Number: Se8
Language: Panoan
Location: The upper Inuya River (10°10′ to 10°30′S, 72° to 72°30′W)
Period: 1960, the date of the beginning of the field work by Carneiro and Dole
Authorities: Carneiro; Dole; Huxley and Capa

171. **Inca**

Sampling Province: 185 (Highland Peru)
Ethnographic Atlas Number: Sf1
Language: Kechumaran (Quechuan)
Location: The Quechua-speaking Indians in the vicinity of Cuzco (13°30′S, 72°W)
Period: 1530, immediately prior to the Spanish conquest
Authorities: Cobo; de Cieza de Leon; Rowe (secondary)

173. **Siriono**

Sampling Province: 187 (Lowland Bolivia)
Ethnographic Atlas Number: Se1
Language: Tupi-Guarani
Location: The forests near the Rio Blanco (14° to 15°S, 63° to 64°W)
Period: 1942, during the period of Holmberg's field work
Authority: Holmberg

174. **Nambicuara**

Sampling Province: 188 (Western Mato Grosso)
Ethnographic Atlas Number: Si4
Language: Nambicuaran
Location: The Cocozu or eastern Nambicuara (12°30′ to 13°30′S, 58°30′ to 59°W)
Period: 1940, shortly prior to the field work of Levi-Strauss
Authority: Levi-Strauss

175. **Trumai**

Sampling Province: 189 (Upper Xingu)
Ethnographic Atlas Number: Si2
Language: Trumaian
Location: The single surviving Trumai village (11°50'S, 53°40'W)
Period: 1938, the date of Quain's field work
Authorities: Murphy and Quain

177. **Tupinamba**

Sampling Province: 191 (Tupi)
Ethnographic Atlas Number: Sj8
Language: Tupi-Guarani
Location: Rio de Janeiro (22°30' to 23°S, 42° to 44°30'W)
Period: 1550, at the time of Staden's captivity
Authorities: Staden, Thevet

178. **Botocudo**

Sampling Province: 192 (East Brazilian Highlands)
Ethnographic Atlas Number: Sj5
Language: Botocudan
Location: The Naknenuk subtribe in the basin of the Rio Doce (18° to
    20°S, 41°30' to 43°30'W)
Period: 1884, the date of Ehrenreich's field work
Authority: Ehrenreich

179. **Sahvante**

Sampling Province: 193 (Upper Araguaya and Tocantins)
Ethnographic Atlas Number: Sj11
Language: Ge
Location: The Akwe-Shavante in the vicinity of Sao Domingos
    (13°30'S, 51°30'W)
Period: 1958, the date of the first field work by Maybury-Lewis
Authority: Maybury-Lewis

181. **Cayua**

Sampling Province: 195 (Guarani)
Ethnographic Atlas Number: Sj10
Language: Tupi-Guarani
Location: Southern Mato Grosso, Brazil (23° to 24°S, 54° to 56°W)
Period: 1890, the approximate period of the earlier good descriptions
Authorities: Watson; Muller

182. **Lengua**

Sampling Province: 196 (Paraguayan Chaco)
Ethnographic Atlas Number: Sh9
Language: Mascoian
Location: The Lengua in contact with the Anglican mission (23° to 24°S, 58° to 59°W)
Period: 1889, the date of the founding of the mission
Authority: Grubb

183. **Abipon**

Sampling Province: 197 (Argentine Chaco)
Ethnographic Atlas Number: Sh3
Language: Guaycuran
Location: The Abipon in contact with the Jesuit mission (27° to 29°S, 59° to 60°W)
Period: 1750, at beginning of Dobrizhoffer's missionary field work
Authority: Dobrizhoffer

185. **Tehuelche**

Sampling Province: 199 (Patagonians)
Ethnographic Atlas Number: Sg4
Language: Tehuelchean
Location: The equestrian Tehuelche (40° to 50°S, 64° to 72°W)
Period: 1870, during the period of field work by Musters
Authority: Musters

186. **Yaghan**

Sampling Province: 200 (Fuegians)
Ethnographic Atlas Number: Sg1
Language: Yaghan
Location: Eastern and central Yaghan (54°30′ to 55°30′S, 67° to 70°W)
Period: 1865, early in the period of missionary field work by Bridges
Authorities: Gusinde; Bridges; Lothrop

Appendix II

DEFINITION OF VARIABLES IN TABLE 5.1

Column 1: World Area. Each of the Murdock and White standard cross-cultural sample societies is part of one of six major world regions. These are, with the number of societies included in each region in the present sample:

A   Sub Saharan Africa (15)
C   Circum-Mediterranean (13)
E   East Eurasia (11)
I   Insular Pacific (12)
N   North America (31)
S   South and Central America (22)

Column 2: Political Autonomy. Societies in the present sample were assigned either of the following codes by Tuden and Marshall (1972).

U   The society is theoretically subject to another society with an alien culture, e.g., to a colonial power, but is in fact essentially unadministered by the latter and thus enjoys *de facto* autonomy.

A   The society or its relevant subgroup is (or was) fully autonomous politically.

Column 3: Hierarchy. This information has been taken directly from Murdock and Provost's (1973) column nine, "level of political integration," which they define as "the number of distinct jurisdictional levels recognizable in the society" (p. 382).

4   Three or more administrative levels are recognized above that of the local community, as in the case of a large state organized into provinces which are subdivided into districts.

3   Two administrative levels are recognized above that of the local community, as in the case of a small state divided into administrative districts.

2   One administrative level is recognized above that of the local community, as in the case of a petty state with a paramount chief ruling over a number of local communities.

1   The society is stateless but is composed of politically organized autonomous local communities.

0   The society is stateless, and political authority is not centralized even on the local level but is dispersed among households or other small component units.

Column 4: Bias in Conflict Resolution. This is a measure of degree of despotism, or the extent to which one individual, at the head of the social hierarchy, is able to exploit his position of strength when a conflict of interest arises, effecting a biased result in his favor. It does not include such asymmetry over slaves, who, as subjugated members of other groups, are disenfranchised members of the simplest societies, or does it include asymmetry over members of a household, within which the head may enjoy a paterfamilistic power over the lives of others. It should also be noted that this definition of despotism differs from that suggested by Carpenter (1971), and employed by Wilson (1975) and others.

1   What bias in the resolution of individual conflicts exists is not extreme, usually being effected by differences in strength, kinship connections, or wealth between the individuals involved. Despotism absent.

2   Conflicts of interest among individuals are resolved with extreme bias, one individual being immune from sanction or even from accusation for major offenses (such as murder) against another, while the other may incur severe punishment, even death, for trivial offenses (such as insult), or for no reason at all. Despotism present.

Column 5: Perquisites. This is a measure of the extent to which individuals in the jurisdictional hierarchy exploit their positions to accrue rewards in the form of fines, fees, bribes, and confiscations, in connection with dispute resolution.

1 Perquisites are small, the reward in a single case being roughly less than a bride price or a bride.

2 Perquisites are substantial, the reward in a single case being roughly greater than or equal to a bride price or a bride.

Column 6: Degree of Polygyny. This is a measure of maximum harem size in a society, the number of simultaneous conjugal relationships with concubines and wives which the individual at the head of the social hierarchy (or, where there is no hierarchy, the most polygynous man) enjoys. Clearly, this measure of degree of polygyny differs from previous cross-cultural codes indicating whether or not a given proportion of group members have more than one "legitimate" spouse (e.g., Murdock, 1957; Murdock and Wilson, 1972; Textor, 1967:24), excluding concubines (Murdock, 1949:26).

1 3 conjugal relationships or less
2 4–10 conjugal relationships
3 11–100 conjugal relationships
4 More than 100 conjugal relationships

BIBLIOGRAPHY

Aberle, D.
1961. Matrilineal descent in cross cultural perspective. *In* D. Schneider and K. Gough, eds. *Matrilineal kinship*, pp. 655–727. Berkeley: University of California Press.

Abugov, R. and Michod, R. E.
1981. On the relation of family structured models and inclusive fitness models for kin selection. *Journal of Theoretical Biology* **88**, 743–754.

Acton, J. E. E. D.
1948. *Essays on freedom and power*. Boston: Beacon Press.

Alexander, R. D.
1971. The search for an evolutionary philosophy of man. *Proceedings of the Royal Society of Victoria* **84**, 99–120.

1974. The evolution of social behavior. *Annual Review of Ecology and Systematics* **5**, 325–383.

1975. The search for a general theory of behavior. *Behavioral Science* **20**, 77–100.

1977. Natural selection and the analysis of human sociality. *In* C. E. Goulden, ed. *Changing scenes in the natural sciences: 1776–1976*. Spec. publ. **12**, 283–337. Bicentennial symposium monograph. Philadelphia, PA: Philosophical Academy of Natural Science.

1978. Natural selection and societal laws. *In* T. Englehardt and D. Callahan, eds. *The foundations of ethics and its relationship to science*, Vol. 3, pp. 138–182. Hastings-on-Hudson, NY: Hastings Institute.

1979. *Darwinism and human affairs*. Seattle: University of Washington Press.

1985. *The biology of moral systems*. In preparation.

Alexander, R. D. and Borgia, G.
1978. Group selection, altruism, and the levels of organization of life. *Annual Review of Ecology and Systematics* **9**, 449–474.

1979. On the origin and basis of the male-female phenomenon. *In* M. F. Blum and N. Blum, eds. *Sexual selection and reproductive competition in insects*, pp. 417–440. New York: Academic Press.

Alexander, R. D., Hoogland, J. L., Howard, R. D., Noonan, K. M., and Sherman, P. W.
1979. Sexual dimorphisms and breeding systems in pinnipeds, ungulates, primates, and humans. *In* N. A. Chagnon and W. Irons, eds. *Evolutionary biology and human social behavior: An anthropological perspective*, pp. 402–435. North Scituate, MA: Duxbury Press.

Alexander, R. D. and Noonan, K. M.
1979. Concealment of ovulation, parental care, and human social evolution. *In* N. A. Chagnon and W. Irons, eds. *Evolutionary biology and human social behavior: An anthropological perspective*, pp. 436–461. North Scituate, MA: Duxbury Press.

Allen, L. L., Bridges, P. S., Evon, D. L., Rosenberg, K. R., Russell, M. D., Schepartz, L. A., Vitzthum, V. J., and Wolpoff, M. H.
  1982. Demography and human origins. *American Anthropologist* **84,** 888–896.

Ammar, H.
  1954. *Growing up in an Egyptian village*. London: Routledge and Kegan Paul.

Anderson, R. G.
  1911. *Some tribal customs in their relation to medicine and morals of the Nyam-Nyam and Gour people inhabiting the eastern Bahr-El-Ghazal*. Wellcome Tropical Research Laboratories at the Gordon Memorial College, Khartoum. Rept. **48.** 239–277.

Ardener, E.
  1962. *Divorce and fertility: An African study*. Nigerian Sociological and Economic Studies, no. 3. London: Oxford.

Armstrong, J. M. and Metraux, A.
  1948. The Goajiro. *In* J. H. Steward, ed. *Handbook of South American indians*, Vol. 4, pp. 369–383. Washington, D. C.: Government Printing Office.

Asch, T. and Chagnon, N. A.
  1975. The Ax Fight. 16mm film. Sommerville, MA: Documentary Educational Resources.

Axelrod, R. M.
  1984. *The evolution of cooperation*. New York: Basic Books.

Axelrod, R. M. and Hamilton, W. D.
  1981. The evolution of cooperation. *Science* **211,** 1390–1396.

Aymonier, E. F.
  1900. *Cambodia, I: The modern kingdom*. Paris: Ernest Leroux. HRAF translation.

Bachofen, J. J.
  1861 [1968]. *Myth, religion, and mother-right: Selected writings of J. J. Bachofen*. London: Routledge and Kegan Paul.

Bailey, A. M. and Llobera, J. R., eds.
  1981. *The asiatic mode of production*. Boston: Routledge and Kegan Paul.

Balsdon, J. P. V. D.
  1962. *Roman women*. London: The Bodley Head.
  1969. *Life and leisure in ancient Rome*. New York: McGraw-Hill.

Bandelier, A. F.
  1880. On the social organization and mode of government of the ancient Mexicans. *American Archaeology and Ethnology* **2,** 557–699.

Barnett, H. G.
  1949. *Palauan society*. Eugene: University of Oregon.
  1979. *Being and Palauan*. New York: Holt, Rinehart, and Winston.

Barry, H. and Paxson, L. M.
  1971. Infancy and early childhood: cross-cultural codes 2. *Ethnology* **10,** 466–508.

Barry, H., Josephson, L., Lauer, E., and Marshall, C.
  1976. Traits inculcated in childhood: cross-cultural codes 5. *Ethnology* **15,** 83–114.

Bateman, A. J.
  1948. Intrasexual selection in *Drosophila*. *Heredity* **2,** 349–368.

Bateson, P.P.G., ed.
  1983. *Mate choice.* London: Cambridge.
Baxter, P. T. W. and Butt, A.
  1953. *The Azande, and related peoples of the Anglo-Egyptian Sudan and Belgian Congo.* London: International African Institute.
Beaton, A. C.
  1948. The Fur. *Sudan Notes and Records* **29**, 1–39.
Becker, G. S.
  1960. An economic analysis of fertility. *In* Universities-National Bureau. *Demographic and economic change in developed countries*, pp. 209–240. Princeton, NJ: Princeton University Press.
  1981. *A treatise on the family.* Cambridge: Harvard University Press.
Benshoof, L. and Thornhill, R.
  1979. The evolution of monogamy and concealed ovulation in humans. *Journal of Social and Biological Structures* **2**, 95–106.
Bernstein, C. and Woodward, R.
  1975. *All the president's men.* New York: Simon and Schuster.
Berté, N. A.
  1982. Some evolutionary implications of K'ekchi' labor transactions. Paper read a symposium at Northwestern University.
  1983. Agricultural production and labor investment strategies in a K'ekchi' Indian village, S. Belize. Ph.D. Dissertation, Northwestern University.
Bertrand, A.
  1899. *The kingdom of the Barotsi.* London: T. F. Unwin.
Best, E.
  1924. *The Maori.* Wellington: H. H. Tombs.
Betzig, L. L.
  1982. Despotism and differential reproduction: a cross cultural correlation of conflict asymmetry, hierarchy, and degree of polygyny. *Ethology and Sociobiology* **3**, 209–221.
  1985. Redistribution: equity or exploitation? *In* L. Betzig, M. Borgerhoff Mulder, and P. Turke, eds. *Human reproductive behavior.* London: Cambridge, in press.
Betzig, L. L. and Turke, P. W.
  1985a. Food sharing on Ifaluk (ms.).
  1985b. Parental investment by sex on Ifaluk. *Ethology and Sociobiology*, in press.
Bigelow, R.
  1971. *The dawn warriors.* Boston: Little, Brown.
Birket-Smith, K. and De Laguna, F.
  1938. *The Eyak indians of the Copper River Delta, Alaska.* Kobenhavn: Levin and Munksgaard. HRAF translation.
Black, D.
  1976. *The behavior of law.* New York: Academic Press.
Bloch, M.
  1983. *Marxism and anthropology: The history of a relationship.* Oxford: Clarendon.
Bohannan, P.
  1957. *Justice and judgement among the Tiv.* London: Oxford.
  1967a. Drumming the scandal among the Tiv. *In* P. Bohannan, ed. *Law and warfare*, pp. 263–265. Garden City: Natural History Press.

1967b. Introduction. *In* P. Bohannan, ed. *Law and warfare*, pp. xi–xiv. Garden City: Natural History Press.

Borgerhoff Mulder, M.

1985. A Darwinian explanation for brideprice among the Kipsigi. *In* L. Betzig, M. Borgerhoff Mulder, and Turke, P. eds. *Human reproductive behavior*. London: Cambridge, in press.

Borgia, G.

1979. Sexual selection and the evolution of mating systems. *In* M. S. Blum and N.A. Blum, eds. *Sexual selection and reproductive competition in insects*, pp. 19–80. New York: Academic Press.

Boserup, E.

1965. *The conditions of agricultural growth*. London: G. Allen and Unwin.

1970. *Women's role in economic development*. London: G. Allen and Unwin.

Bowers, A. W.

1965. *Hidatsa social and ceremonial organization*. Bureau of American Ethnology, Bulletin 194.

Boulanger, N. A.

1764. *The origin and progress of despotism in the oriental, and other empires, of Africa, Europe, and America*. Amsterdam.

Boyd, R. and Richerson, P. J.

1982. Cultural transmission and the evolution of cooperative behavior. *Human Ecology* **10**, 325–351.

Briggs, L. P.

1951. The ancient Khmer empire. *American Philosophical Society, Transactions* **41**, 237–250.

Brock, R. G. C.

1918. Some notes on the Zande tribe as found in the Meridi district. *Sudan Notes and Records* **1**, 249–262.

Broude, G. J. and Greene, S. J.

1976. Cross-cultural codes on twenty sexual attitudes and practices. *Ethnology* **15**, 409–429.

Burling, R.

1962. Maximization theories and the study of economic anthropology. *American Anthropologist* **64**, 802–821.

Burton, M. L. and White, D. R.

1985. Distance (DISTAN), language (LINGUA), and political influence (EMPIRE) autocorrelation matricies. *World Cultures*, in press.

Bury, J. B.

1923. *History of the latter Roman Empire*. New York: Dover.

Cabello y Robles, D.

1961. A description of the Comanche Indians in 1786 by the governor of Texas. *West Texas Historical Association, Yearbook* **37**, 177–182.

Cain, M.

1977. The economic activities of children in a village in Bangladesh. *Population and Development Review* **3**, 201–227.

Caldwell, J. C.

1977. The economic rationality of high fertility: an investigation illustrated with Nigerian survey data. *Population Studies* **31**, 5–27.

Campbell, B., ed.

1972. *Sexual selection and the descent of man 1871–1971*. New York: Aldine.

Cantor, N. F.
1969. *Medieval history*, 2nd edition. London: Macmillan.
Carcopino, J.
1940. *Daily life in ancient Rome*. New Haven: Yale University Press.
Carneiro, R. L.
1970. A theory of the origin of the state. *Science* **169**, 733–738.
Carpenter, C. C.
1971. Discussion of session I: territoriality and dominance. *In* A. H. Esser, ed. *Behavior and environment*, pp. 46–47. New York: Plenum Press.
Casati, G.
1891. The Sandeh. *In* G. Casati and E. Pasha, ed. *Ten years in equatoria and return*. London: Frederick Warne.
Chagnon, N. A.
1968a. The culture-ecology of shifting (pioneering) cultivation among the Yanomamo Indians. Reprinted *In* D. Gross, ed. *The cultural ecology of South American indians*, pp. 126–142. Garden City: Natural History Press.
1968b. Yanomamo social organization and warfare. *In* M. Fried, M. Harris, and R. Murphy, eds. *War: The anthropology of armed conflict and aggression*, pp. 109-159. Garden City: Natural History Press.
1972. Social causes for population fissioning: tribal social organization and genetic microdifferentiation. *In* G. A. Harrison and A. J. Boyce, eds. *The structure of human populations*, pp. 252–282. Oxford: Clarendon.
1974. *Studying the Yanomamo*. New York: Holt, Rinehart and Winston.
1975. Genealogy, solidarity and relatedness: Limits to local group size and patterns of fissioning in an expanding population. *Yearbook of Physical Anthropology* **19**, 95–110.
1979a. Is reproductive success equal in egalitarian societies? *In* N. A. Chagnon and W. Irons, eds. *Evolutionary biology and human social behavior: An anthropological perspective*, pp. 374–402. North Scituate, MA: Duxbury Press.
1979b. Mate competition, favoring close kin, and village fissioning among the Yanomamo Indians. *In* N. A. Chagnon and W. Irons, eds. *Evolutionary biology and human social behavior: An anthropological perspective*, pp. 95–110. North Scituate, MA: Duxbury Press.
1980. Kin selection theory, kinship, marriage and fitness among the Yanomamo Indians. *In* G. W. Barlow and J. Silverberg, eds. *Sociobiology: Beyond nature nurture?* AAAS Selected Symposium No. 35. pp. 545–571. Boulder: Westview Press.
1981. Terminological kinship, genealogical relatedness, and village fissioning among the Yanomamo Indians. *In* R. D. Alexander and D. W. Tinkle, eds. *Natural selection and social behavior: Recent research and new theory*, pp. 490–508. New York: Chiron.
1982. Sociodemographic attributes of nepotism in tribal populations: man the rule breaker. *In* King's College Sociobiology Group, ed. *Current problems in sociobiology*, pp. 291–318. London: Cambridge University Press.
1983. *Yanamamo: The fierce people*, 3rd edition. New York: Holt, Rinehart, and Winston.
Chagnon, N. A. and Bugos, P.
1979. Kin selection and conflict: an analysis of a Yanomamo ax fight. *In* N. A. Chagnon and W. Irons, eds. *Evolutionary biology and human social behavior: An anthropological perspective*, pp. 213–237. North Scituate, MA: Duxbury Press.

Chen, K-H, Cavalli-Sforza, L. L. and Feldman, M. W.
    1982. A study of cultural transmission in Taiwan. *Human Ecology* **10**,
    365–382.
Chester, R., ed.
    1977. *Divorce in Europe.* Publications of the Netherlands Interuniversity
    Institute and Population and Family Study Center, Vol. 3.
Childs, G. M.
    1949. *Umbundu kinship and character.* London: International African
    Institute.
Cieza de Leon, P. de
    1959. *The Incas.* Norman: University of Oklahoma.
Clignet, R.
    1970. *Many wives many powers.* Evanston: Northwestern University Press.
Clutton-Brock, T. H., Guinness, F. E., and Albon, S. D.
    1982. *Red deer: The behavior and ecology of two sexes.* Chicago: University
    of Chicago Press.
Cohen, R.
    1971. *Dominance and defiance: A study of marital instability in an Islamic
    African society.* Washington, D. C.: American Anthropological Associa-
    tion.
Coon, C. S.
    1931. *Tribes of the Rif.* Peabody Museum of American Archeology and
    Ethnology, No. 18.
    1950. *The mountain of giants.* Peabody Museum of American Archaeology
    and Ethnology, Vol. 23, No. 3.
Cooper, J. M.
    1946. The Yaghan. *In* J. H. Steward, ed. *Handbook of South American
    indians,* Vol. 1, pp. 81–106. Washington, D. C.: Government Printing
    Office.
Crook, W. P.
    n. d. Selection from Shehan, G. M., *Marquesan source materials.* Ms. at
    Cumulative Cross Cultural Coding Center, University of Pittsburgh.
Cushing, F. H.
    1882. The nation of the willows. *Atlantic Monthly* **50**, 362–374; 541–559.
Czekanowski, J.
    1924. *Researches in the region between the Nile and the Congo,* Vol. 2.
    Leipzig: Klinkhardt und Biermann. HRAF translation.
Daly, M.
    1982. Some caveats about cultural transmission models. *Human Ecology*
    10, 401–408.
Daly, M. and Wilson, M.
    1981. Abuse and neglect of children in evolutionary perspective. *In* R. D.
    Alexander and D. W. Tinkle, eds. *Natural selection and social behavior:
    Recent research and new theory,* pp. 405–416. New York: Chiron.
    1982. Homicide and kinship. *American Anthropologist* **84**, 372–378.
    1983. *Sex, evolution, and behavior,* 2nd edition. Boston: Willard Grant.
Daly, M., Wilson, M., and Weghorst, S. J.
    1982. Male sexual jealousy. *Ethology and Sociobiology* **3**, 11–27.
Darwin, C. R.
    1859. *The origin of species.* New York: Random House. (Modern Library
    edition published with *The descent of man and selection in relation to sex,*
    pp. 1–386.)

1871. *The descent of man and selection in relation to sex.* New York: Random House. (Modern Library edition published with *The origin of species*, pp. 387–1000.)

Dawkins, R.

1976. *The selfish gene.* London: Oxford.

1982. *The extended phenotype: The gene as the unit of selection.* Oxford: W. H. Freeman.

Day, L. H.

1963. Divorce in Australia. *Australian Quarterly* **35,** 57–66.

De Fries, J. C. and McClearn, G. E.

1970. Social dominance and Darwinian fitness in the laboratory mouse. *American Naturalist* **104,** 408–411.

Denys, N.

1908. *The description and natural history of the coasts of North America.* Toronto: Champlaign Society.

De Pineda, R.

1950. *Aspects of magic in La Guajira.* HRAF translation.

De Vaux, R.

1961. *Ancient Israel.* London: Darton, Longman, and Todd.

Dewsbury, D. A.

1982. Dominance rank, copulatory behavior, and differential reproduction. *Quarterly Review of Biology* **57,** 135–159.

Diaz del Castillo, B.

1910. *The true history of the conquest of New Spain,* Vol. 2. London: Hakluyt Society.

Dickemann, M.

1979a. Female infanticide, reproductive strategies, and social stratification: a preliminary model. *In* N. A. Chagnon and W. Irons, eds. *Evolutionary biology and human social behavior: An anthropological perspective,* pp. 321–367. North Scituate, MA: Duxbury Press.

1979b. The ecology of mating systems in hypergynous dowry societies. *Social Science Information* **18,** 163–195.

1981. Paternal confidence and dowry competition: a biocultural analysis of purdah. *In* R. D. Alexander and D. W. Tinkle, eds. *Natural selection and social behavior: Recent research and new theory,* pp. 417–438. New York: Chiron.

Dill, S.

1925. *Roman society from Nero to Marcus Aurelius.* London: MacMillan.

Dorsey, G. A. and Murie, J. R.

1940. *Notes on Skidi Pawnee society.* Chicago: Field Museum.

Dow, M. M.

1984. A biparametric approach to network autocorrelation. *Sociological Methods and Research* **13,** 201–217.

1985. Agricultural intensification and craft specialization: A nonrecursive model. *Ethnology* **24,** 137–152.

Dow, M. M., Burton, M. L., and White, D. R.

1982. Network autocorrelation: a simulation study of a foundational problem in regression and survey research. *Social Networks* **4,** 169–200.

Dow, M. M., Burton, M. L., White, D. R., and Reitz, K. P.

1984. Galton's problem as network autocorrelation. *American Ethnologist* **11,** 754–770.

Dow, M. M., Burton, M. L., White, D. R., and Reitz, K. P.
    1984. Galton's problem as network autocorrelation. *American Ethnologist* **11,** 754–770.
Dow, M. M., White, D. R., and Burton, M. L.
    1984. Multivariate modeling with interdependent network data. *Behavior Science Research* **17,** 216–245.
Driver, G. R. and Miles, J. C.
    1955. *The Babylonian laws.* Oxford: Clarendon.
Driver, H. E.
    1956. An integration of functional, evolutionary, and historical theory by means of correlations. Indiana University Publications in Anthropology and Linguistics, *Memoir* **12,** 1–35.
Dunbar, R. I. M.
    1982. Adaptation, fitness, and the evolutionary tautology. *In* King's College Sociobiology Group, ed. *Current problems in sociobiology,* pp. 9–28. London: Cambridge.
Duncan, J.
    1847. *Travels in Western Africa in 1845 and 1846, comprising a journey from Waydah through the kingdom of Dahomey to Adofoodin.* London: Richard Bentley.
Dunn, S. P.
    1982. *The fall and rise of the asiatic mode of production.* London: Routledge and Kegan Paul.
Dupré, G. and Rey, P-P.
    n. d. Theory of the history of exchange, with an example from the Western Congo.
Durham, M. E.
    1928. *Some tribal origins, laws and customs of the Balkans.* London: George Allen and Unwin.
Durham, W. H.
    1979. Toward a coevolutionary theory of human biology and culture. *In* N. A. Chagnon and W. Irons, eds. *Evolutionary biology and human social behavior: An anthropological perspective,* pp. 39–59. North Scituate, Mass.: Duxbury Press.
    1982. Interactions of genetic and cultural evolution: models and examples. *Human Ecology* **10,** 289–323.
Durkheim, E.
    1933 [1893]. *The division of labor in society.* New York: The Free Press.
    1966 [1895]. *The rules of sociological method.* New York: The Free Press.
Du Tetre, J. B.
    1667. *General history of the Antilles occupied by the French,* Vol. 2. Paris: T. Iolly. HRAF translation.
East, R., ed.
    1939. *Akiga's story: The Tiv tribe as seen by one of its members.* London: Oxford.
Easterlin, R. A.
    1975. An economic framework for fertility analysis. *Studies in Family Planning* **6,** 54–63.
Eglar, Z.
    1960. *A Punjabi village in Pakistan.* New York: Columbia University Press.

Ehrlich, E.
    1936. *Fundamental principles of the sociology of law*. Cambridge: Harvard.
Elmendorf, W. W.
    1960. *The structure of Twana culture*. Washington State University Mono-
    graphic Suppl. No.2. Pullman, Wash.: Washington State University Press.
Ember, M.
    1974. Warfare, sex ratio, and polygyny. *Ethnology* **13**, 197–206.
Emlen, S. T. and Oring, L. W.
    1977. Ecology, sexual selection, and the evolution of mating systems.
    Science **197**, 215–223.
Engels, F.
    1884 [1964]. *The origin of the family, private property, and the state*. New
    York: International Publishers.
    1890 [1980]. Letter to J. Bloch. In K. Marx and F. Engels, *Selected works*, pp.
    692–639. New York: International Publishers.
Essock-Vitale, S. M.
    1984. The reproductive success of wealthy Americans. *Ethology and So-
    ciobiology* **5**, 45–49.
Essock-Vitale, S. M. and McGuire, M.T.
    1980. Predictions derived from the theories of kin selection and recipro-
    cation, assessed by anthropological data. *Ethology and Sociobiology* **1**,
    233–243.
    1985. Patterns of helping among Los Angeles women. *Ethology and Soci-
    obiology*, in press.
Evans Pritchard, E. E.
    1940. *The Nuer*. Oxford: Clarendon.
    1971. *The Azande: History and political institutions*. Oxford: Clarendon.
Fedigan, L. M.
    1983. Dominance and reproductive success in primates. *Yearbook of Phys-
    ical Anthropology* **26**, 91–129.
Felkin, R. W.
    1885. Notes on the Fur Tribe of Central Africa. *Proceedings of the Royal
    Society of Edinburgh* **13**, 205–265.
Filipovitch, M. J.
    1958. Vicarious paternity among the Serbs and Croats. *Southwestern Jour-
    nal of Anthropology* **14**, 156–167.
Firth, R. W.
    1936. *We, the Tikopia* London: Allen and Unwin.
    1939. *Primitive polynesian economy*. London: George Routledge.
    1949. Authority and public opinion in Tikopia. *In* M. Fortes, ed. *Social
    structure: Studies presented to A. R. Radcliffe-Brown*, pp. 168–188. Ox-
    ford: Clarendon.
    1951. *Elements of social organization*. London: Watts.
    1959. *Social change in Tikopia: Re-study of a polynesian community after
    a generation*. London: Allen and Unwin.
Fisher, R. A.
    1930 [1958, 2nd edition]. *The genetical theory of natural selection*. New
    York: Dover.
Flannery, K. V.
    1972. The cultural evolution of civilizations. *Annual Review of Ecology
    and Systematics* **3**, 399–426.

Flannery, R.
    1953. *The Gros Ventres of Montana. Part 1, Social life.* Washington, D. C.:
    Catholic University of America.
Fletcher, A. C. and La Flesche, F.
    1906. *The Omaha tribe.* Bureau of American Ethnology, Bulletin No. 27.
Flinn, M. V.
    1981. Uterine versus agnatic kinship variability and associated cousin
    marriage preferences: an evolutionary biological analysis. *In* R. D. Alexan-
    der and D. W. Tinkle, eds. *Natural selection and social behavior: Recent
    research and new theory,* pp. 439–475. New York: Chiron.
    1983. Resources, mating, and kinship: the behavioral ecology of a Trin-
    idadian Village. Ph.D. Dissertation, Northwestern University.
Flinn, M. V. and Alexander, R. D.
    1982. Cuture theory: the developing synthesis from biology. *Human Ecol-
    ogy* **10,** 383–400.
Fortes, M.
    1959. Descent, filiation, and affinity: a rejoinder to Dr. Leach. *Man* **59,**
    193–197, 206–212.
Fredlund, E. V.
    1985. Who commits "incest" among the Yanomamo? *Ethology and Soci-
    obiology,* in press.
Freeman, D.
    1983. *Margaret Mead and Samoa: The making and unmaking of an an-
    thropological myth.* Cambridge: Harvard Univ. Press.
Fried, M. M.
    1967. *The evolution of political society.* New York: Random House.
Friedlander, L.
    1908. *Roman life and manners under the early empire.* London: Routledge
    and Sons.
Garcilaso de la Vega
    1609–1617 [1871]. *Royal commentaries of the Yncas.* London: Hakluya
    Society. Also [1961]. New York: Orians Press.
Garnsey, P.
    1968. Legal privilege in the Roman Empire. *Past and Present* **31,** 3–24.
    1970. *Social status and legal privilege in the Roman empire.* Oxford:
    Clarendon.
Gaulin, S. J. C. and Fitzgerald, R. W.
    1985. Sex differences in spatial ability: an evolutionary hypothesis and
    test. *American Naturalist,* in press.
Gaulin, S. J. C. and Schlegel, A.
    1980. Paternal confidence and parental investment: a cross cultural test of
    a sociobiological hypothesis. *Ethology and Sociobiology* **1,** 301–309.
Gayton, A. H.
    1948. *Yokuts and western Mono ethnography.* Berkeley: University of
    California Press.
Ghieselin, M.
    1969. *The triumph of the Darwinian method.* Berkeley: University of
    California Press.
Gluckman, M.
    1950. Kinship and marriage among the Lozi of Northern Rhodesia and the
    Zulu of Natal. *In* A. R. Radcliffe-Brown and D. Forde, eds. *African systems
    of kinship and marriage,* pp. 166–206. London: Oxford.

1965. *The judicial process among the Barotse of northern Rhodesia.* Manchester: Manchester University Press.

1972. *The ideas in Barotse jurisprudence.* Manchester: Manchester University Press.

Godelier, M.

1978. The concept of the 'Asiatic mode of production' and Marxist models of social evolution. *In* D. Seddon, ed. *Relations of production,* pp. 209–257. Totowa, NJ: Frank Cass.

1981. On the Asiatic mode of production. *In* A. M. Bailey and J. R. Llobera, eds. *The asiatic mode of production.* Boston: Routledge and Kegan Paul.

Goodenough, R. G.

1970. Adoption on Romonum, Truk. *In* V. Carroll, ed. *Adoption in Eastern Oceania,* pp. 314–340. Honolulu: University of Hawaii Press.

Goody, J.

1976. *Production and reproduction.* London: Cambridge.

Gould, S. J.

1980. *The Panda's thumb.* New York: Norton.

Gouldsbury, C. and Sharpe, A.

1911. *The great plateau of Northern Rhodesia.* London: Edward Arnold.

Greene, P.

1978. Promiscuity, paternity, and culture. *American Ethnologist* **5,** 151–159.

Gruhl, M.

1935. *The citadel of Ethiopia: The empire of the divine emperor.* London: Jonathan Cape.

Gruter, M. and Bohannan, P., eds.

1982. *Law, biology and culture.* Proceedings of the first Monterrey Dunes Conferences. *Journal of Social and Biological Structures,* **5.**

Guhl, A. M. and Fischer, G. J.

1969. The behavior of chickens. *In* E. S. E. Hafez, ed. *The behaviour of domestic animals,* pp. 515–553. Baltimore: Williams and Wilkins.

Gusinde, M.

1937. *The Yaghan: The life and thought of the water nomads of Cape Horn.* Modling bei Wien: Anthropos-Bibliothek. HRAF translation.

Haldane, J. B. S.

1932. *The causes of evolution,* Reprint edition, 1966. Ithaca: Cornell University Press.

Hallowell, A. I.

1955. *Culture and experience.* Philadelphia: Univ. of Pennsylvania Press.

Hallpike, C. R.

1972. *The Konso of Ethiopia.* Oxford: Clarendon.

Hambly, W. D.

1934. Occupational ritual, belief, and custom among the Ovimbundu. *American Anthropologist* **36,** 157–167.

Hames, R. B.

1979. Relatedness and interaction among the Ye'kwana: a preliminary analysis. *In* N. A. Chagnon and W. Irons, eds. *Evolutionary biology and human social behavior: An anthropological perspective,* pp. 238–249. North Scituate, Mass.: Duxbury Press.

1982. Exchange balance and relatedness in Ye'kwana gardening. Paper read at a symposium at Northwestern University.

Hamilton, W. D.
   1963. The evolution of altruistic behavior. *American Naturalist* **97,** 354–356.
   1964. The genetical evolution of social behavior, I, II. *Journal of Theoretical Biology* **7,** 1–52.
Hamilton, W. D. and Zuk, M.
   1982: Heritable true fitness and bright birds: a role for parasites? *Science* **218,** 384–387.
Handy, E. S. C.
   1923. *Marquesan somatology.* London.
Hardin, G.
   1968. The tragedy of the commons. *Science* **162,** 1243–1248.
Harner, M. J.
   1968. Population pressure and the social evolution of agriculturalists. *Southwestern Journal of Anthropology* **26,** 67–86.
   1972. *The Jivaro.* Garden City: Natural History Press.
Harris, M.
   1979. *Cultural materialism.* New York: Random House.
Hart, C. W. M. and Pilling, A. R.
   1960. *The Tiwi of north Australia.* New York: Holt, Rinehart and Winston.
Hartung, J.
   1976. On natural selection and the inheritance of wealth. *Current Anthropology* **17,** 607–622.
   1982. Polygyny and the inheritance of wealth. *Current Anthropology* **23,** 1–12.
Hasluck, M.
   1954. *The unwritten law in Albania.* London: Cambridge.
Havlicek, L. L. and Peterson, N. L.
   1974. Robustness of the *t* test: A guide for researchers on effect of violations of assumptions. *Psychological Reports* **34,** 1095–1114.
   1977. Effect of the violation of assumptions upon significance levels of the Pearson *r. Psychological Bulletin* **84,** 373–377.
Heath, D. B.
   1958. Sexual division of labor and cross-cultural research. *Social Forces* **37,** 77–79.
Hecht, A.
   1980. *The Venetian vespers.* New York: Atheneum.
Heizer, R. F. and Mills, J. E.
   1932. *The four ages of Tsurai: A documentary history of the indian village on Trinidad Bay.* Berkeley: University of California Press.
Herskovits, M. J.
   1938. *Dahomey: An ancient west African kingdom.* New York: J. J. Augustin.
Herskovits, M. J. and Herskovits, F. S.
   1934. *Rebel dynasty: Among the bush negroes of Dutch Guiana.* New York: McGraw-Hill.
Hobbes, T.
   1651 [1887]. *Leviathan.* London: George Routledge and Sons.
Hoebel, E. A.
   1940. *The political organization and law-ways of the Comanche indians.* Menasha, Wis.: American Anthropological Association.

1954. *The law of primitive man.* Cambridge: Harvard.

1967. Song duels among the Eskimo. *In* P. Bohanan, ed. *Law and warfare,* pp. 255-262. Garden City: Natural History Press.

1969. Plains Indian law in development: the Comanche. *In* D. R. Cressey and D. A. Ward, eds. *Delinquency, crime, and social process,* pp. 67–78. New York: Harper and Row.

1982. Anthropology, law, and genetic inheritance. *Journal of social and Biological Structures* **5,** 335–339.

Hollis, A. C.

1905. *The Masai: Their language and folklore.* Oxford: Clarendon.

Holmberg, A. R.

1950. *Nomads of the long bow: The Siriono of Eastern Bolivia.* Washington, D. C.: Government Printing Office.

Honigmann, J. J.

1954. *The Kaska indians: An ethnographic reconstruction.* New Haven: Yale Univ. Press.

Hopkins, K.

1978. *Conquerors and slaves.* London: Cambridge.

Hrdy, S. B.

1981. *The woman that never evolved.* Cambridge: Harvard.

Hughes, A. L.

1982. Confidence of paternity and wife sharing in polygynous and polyandrous systems. *Ethology and Sociobiology* **3,** 125–129.

Huntingford, G. W. B.

1955. *The Galla of Ethiopia. In* D. Forde, ed. *Ethnographic survey of Africa, northeastern Africa,* part II. London: International African Institute.

Hurd, J.

1983. Kin relatedness and church fissioning in the "Nebraska" Amish. *Social Biology* **30,** 59–66.

Huttereau, A.

1909. *Notes on the family and legal life of some peoples of the Belgian Congo.* Bruxelles: Ministre des Colonies. HRAF translation.

Huxley, M. and Capa, C.

1964. *Farewell to eden.* New York: Harper and Row.

Irons, W.

1979a. Cultural and biological success. *In* N. A. Chagnon and W. Irons, eds. *Evolutionary biology and human social behavior: An anthropological perspective,* pp.257–272. North Scituate, Mass.: Duxbury Press.

1979b. Political stratification among pastoral nomads. *In Pastoral production and society.* London: Cambridge.

1983. Human female reproductive strategies. *In* S. K. Wasser, ed. *Social behavior of female vertebrates.* pp, 169–213. New York: Academic Press.

James, G. W.

1903. *The Indians of the painted desert region: Hopis, Navahoes, Wallapais, Havasupais.* Boston: Little, Brown.

Jenness, D.

1922. *The life of the Copper Eskimo.* Ottawa: F. A. Acland.

Jenni, D. A.

1974. Evolution of polyandry in birds. *American Zoologist* **14,** 129–144.

Kagwa, A.

1934. *The customs of the Baganda.* New York: Columbia University Press.

Kahn, M. C.
  1931. *Djuka: The bush negroes of Dutch Guiana.* New York: Viking Press.
Karsten, R.
  1949. *A totalitarian state of the past: The civilization of the ancient Inca empire in ancient Peru.* Societies Scientarum Fennica, Commentationes Humanarum Litterarum, XVI.
Kopytoff, I.
  1961. Extension of conflict as a method of conflict resolution among the Suku of the Congo. *Journal of Conflict Resolution* **5,** 61–69.
  1965. The Suku. *In* J. L. Gibbs, ed. *Peoples of Africa,* pp. 441–477. New York: Holt, Rinehart and Winston.
Krader, L.
  1975. *The asiatic mode of production.* Assen: van Gorcum.
Kroeber, A. L.
  1917. The superorganic. *American Anthropologist* **19,** 163–213.
  1925. *Handbook of the indians of California.* Washington, D. C.: Government Printing Office.
Kummer, H.
  1968. *Social organization of hamadryas baboons.* Chicago: University of Chicago Press.
Kurland, J. A.
  1979. Paternity, mother's brother, and human sociality. *In* N. A. Chagnon and W. Irons, eds. *Evolutionary biology and human social behavior: An anthropological perspective,* pp. 145–180. North Scituate, Mass.: Duxbury Press.
  1980. Kin selection theory: A review and selective bibliography. *Ethology and Sociobiology* **1,** 255–274.
La Barre, R. W.
  1934. *Marquesan culture.* Ms. at Cumulative Cross Cultural Coding Center, University of Pittsburgh.
Lagae, C. R.
  1926. *The Azande of Niam-Niam.* Bruxelles: Vromant. HRAF translation.
Lambert, B.
  1966. The economic activities of a Gilbertese chief. *In* M. J. Schwartz *et al.,* eds. *Political anthropology,* pp. 155–172. New York: Aldine.
  1970. Adoption, guardianship, and social stratification in the Northern Gilbert Islands. *In* V. Carroll, ed. *Adoption in eastern Oceania,* pp. 261–291. Honolulu: University of Hawaii Press.
Lane, R. B. and Lane, B. S.
  n.d. Untitled ms. at Cumulative Cross Cultural Coding Center, University of Pittsburgh.
Lange, W.
  1967. *Dialectics of divine kingship in the Kafa Highlands.* Los Angeles: University of California Press.
Leach, E. R.
  1957. Aspects of bridewealth and marriage stability among the Kachin and Lakher. *Man* **57,** 50–55.
  1961. *Rethinking anthropology.* New York: Humanities Press.
Le Boeuf, B. J.
  1974. Male-male competition and reproductive success in elephant seals. *American Zoologist* **14,** 163–176.

Lee, R. B.
  1979. *The !Kung San*. London: Cambridge.
Lee, R. B. and De Vore, I., eds.
  1968. *Man the hunter*. New York: Aldine.
Leigh, E.
  1971. *Adaptation and diversity*. San Francisco: Freeman, Cooper, and Co.
  1977. How does selection reconcile individual advantage with the good of the group? *Proceedings, National Academy of Sciences* **74**, 4542–4546.
Levi-Strauss, C.
  1944. The social and psychological aspect of chieftainship in a primitive tribe: the Nambikwara of Northwestern Mato Grosso. *Transactions New York Academy of Sciences* **7**, 16–32.
  1948. *Family and social life of the Nambikwara indians*. Paris: Societe des Americanistes. HRAF translation.
  1949. *The elementary structures of kinship*. Boston: Beacon Press.
Lewontin, R. C.
  1970. The units of selection. *Annual Review of Ecology and Systematics* **1**, 1–18.
Lewontin, R. C., Rose, S., and Kamin, L. J.
  1984. *Not in our genes*. New York: Pantheon Press.
Lightcap, J. L., Kurland, J. A., and Burgess, R. L.
  1982. Child abuse: a test of some predictions from evolutionary theory. *Ethology and Sociobiology* **3**, 61–67.
Lin, Y.
  1947. *The Lolo of Liang-Shan*. Shanghai: The Commercial Press. HRAF translation.
Linton, R.
  1933. *The Tanala, a hill tribe of Madagascar*. Field Museum of Natural History, Anthropological Series, Vol. 22.
  1939. Marquesan culture. *In* A. Kardiner, ed. *The individual and his society: The psychodynamics of primitive social organization*, pp. 138–196. New York: Columbia University Press.
Llewellyn, K. N. and Hoebel, E. A.
  1941. *The Cheyenne way: Conflict and case law in primitive jurisprudence*. Norman: University of Oklahoma Press.
Loeb, E. M.
  1926. *Pomo folkways*. Berkeley: University of California Press.
Loftin, C.
  1972. Galton's problem as spatial autocorrelation. *Ethnology* **9**, 425–435.
Lovejoy, C. E.
  1981. The origin of man. *Science* **211**, 341–350.
Maccoby, E. E. and Jacklin, C. N.
  1974. *The psychology of sex differences*. Palo Alto: Stanford Univ. Press.
McCulloch, M.
  1952. *The Ovimbundu of Angola*. London: International African Institute.
McIlwraith, T. F.
  1948. *The Bella Coola indians*. Toronto: University of Toronto Press.
McLennan, J. F.
  1865 [1970]. *Primitive marriage*. Chicago: University of Chicago Press.
MacMichael, H. A.
  1922. *A history of the arabs in the Sudan*. London: Cambridge.

Maguire, R. A. J.
    1928. The Masai penal code. *African Society*. **26**, 12–18.
Maine, H. S.
    1864. *Ancient law*. New York: Charles Scribner.
Malinowski, B.
    1922. *Argonauts of the Western Pacific*. New York: Dutton.
    1926 [1982]. *Crime and custom in savage society*. Totowa, NJ: Littlefield,
    Adams, and Co.
Malthus, T. R.
    1798 [1983]. *Essay on population*. Ann Arbor: University of Michigan
    Press.
Marshall, K. M.
    1976. Solidarity or sterility? Adoption and fosterage on Namoluk Atoll. *In*
    I. Brady, ed. *Transactions in kinship*, pp. 28–50. Honolulu: University of
    Hawaii Press.
Marshall, L.
    1959. Marriage among !Kung Bushmen. *Africa* **29**, 335–364.
Marx, K.
    1857–1858 [1973]. *Grundrisse*. New York: Vinatge Books.
    1859 [1980]. Preface to *The critique of political economy*. *In* K. Marx and
    F. Engels, *Selected works*, pp. 181–185. New York: International Publ.
Marx, K. and Engels, F.
    1845 [1976]. *The German ideology*. Part I: Feuerbach. *In* K. Marx and F.
    Engels. *Collected words*, Vol. 5, pp. 27–96. London: Lawrence and Wishert.
Masters, R. D.
    1977. Human nature, natures, and political thought. *In* J. R. Pennock and J.
    W. Chapman, eds. *Human nature in politics*, pp. 69–110. New York: New
    York University Press.
    1978. Of marmots and men: animal behavior and human altruism. *In* L.
    Wispa, ed. *Altruism, sympathy, and helping: Psychology and sociological
    principles*, pp. 59–77. New York: Academic Press.
Mauss, M.
    1925 [1967]. *The gift*. New York: Norton.
Maybury-Lewis, D.
    1967. *Akwe-Shavante society*. Oxford: Clarendon.
Maynard Smith, J.
    1964. Group selection and kin selection. *Nature (London)* **201**, 1145–1147.
Mayr, E.
    1961. Cause and effect in biology. *Science* **134**, 1501–1506.
Meillassoux, C.
    1964. *The economic anthropology of the Guro*. Paris: Mouton.
Merker, M.
    1910. *The Masai: Ethnographic monograph of an east Asian semite people*.
    Berlin: Dietrich Reimer. HRAF translation.
Moore, J.
    1984. The evolution of reciprocal sharing. *Ethology and Sociobiology* **5**,
    5–14.
Moore, S. F.
    1958. *Power and property in Inca Peru*. New York: Columbia University
    Press.

Morgan, L. H.

1871. Systems of consanguinity and affinity of the human family. *Smithsonian contributions to Knowledge* **17**, 4–602.

1877 [1978]. *Ancient society*. Palo Alto: New York Labor News.

Mueller, E.

1976. The economic value of children in peasant agriculture. *In* R. G. Ridker, ed. *Population and development*, pp. 98–153. Baltimore: Johns Hopkins University Press.

Murdock, G. P.

1934. *Our primitive contemporaries*. New York: Macmillan.,

1949. *Social structure*. New York: The Free Press.

1957. World ethnographic sample.*American Anthropologist* **59**, 644–687.

1967. Ethnographic atlas. *Ethnology* **6**, 109–236.

1972. Anthropology's mythology. *Proceedings of the Royal Anthropological Institute of Great Britain and Ireland*, pp. 17–24.

Murdock, G. P. and Morrow, D. O.

1970. Subsistence economy and supportive practices: cross-cultural codes 1. *Ethnology* 9, 302-330.

Murdock, G. P. and Provost, C.

1973. Factors in the division of labor by sex: a cross-cultural analysis. *Ethnology* **12**, 203–225.

Murdock, G. P. and White, D. R.

1969. Standard cross-cultural sample. *Ethnology* **8**, 329–369.

Murdock, G. P. and Wilson, S. F.

1972. Settlement patterns and community organization: cross-cultural codes 3. *Ethnology* **11**, 254–297.

Murphy, R. F. and Quain, B.

1955. *The Trumai indians of central Brazil*. Locust Valley, New York: J. J. Augustin.

Musil, A.

1928. *The manners and customs of the Rwala bedouins*. New York: American Geographical Society.

Musters, G. C.

1873. *At home with the Patagonians*. London: John Murray.

Nadel, S. F.

1947. *The Nuba*. London: Oxford.

Nader, L. and Todd, H. F., eds.

1978. *The disputing process: Law in ten societies*. New York: Columbia University Press.

Nag, M., White, B. and Peet, R.

1978. An anthropological approach to the study of the economic value of children in Java and Nepal. *Current Anthropology* **19**, 293–306.

Naroll, R.

1976. Galton's problem and HRAFLIB. *Behavior Science Research* **11**, 123–148.

National Center for Health Statistics

1977. *Vital statistics of the United States*, Vol. 3, Marriage and Divorce. Washington, D. C.: Government Printing Office.

Needham, R.

1962. *Structure and sentiment*. Chicago: University of Chicago Press.

Niblack, A. P.
    1888. *The coast indians of southern Alaska and northern British Colum-bia.* Annual Report of the Smithsonian Institution, Vol. 2.
Nicolaisen, J.
    1959. Political systems of pastoral Tuareg in Air and Ahaggar. *Folk* **1**, 67–131.
Noth, M.
    1958. *The history of Israel.* New York: Harper and Row.
Opler, M. E.
    1941. *An Apache life-way: The economic, social, and religious institutions of the Chiricahua.* Chicago: University of Chicago Press.
Orians, G. H.
    1969. On the evolution of mating systems in birds and mammals. *American Naturalist* **103**, 589–603.
Osgood, C.
    1951. *The Koreans and their culture.* New York: The Ronald Press.
    1958. *Ingalik social culture.* Yale University publications in anthropology, No. 53. New Haven: Yale.
Paige, K. E. and Paige, J. M.
    1981. *The politics of reproductive ritual.* Berkeley: University of California Press.
Park, W. Z.
    1937. *Shamanism in western North America.* Evanston: Northwestern.
Polo de Ondegardo, J.
    1916. *Information concerning the religion and government of the Incas.* HRAF translation.
Poma de Ayala, F. G.
    1936. *The first new chronicle and good government.* Paris: Institut d'Ethnologie. HRAF translation.
Porter, D.
    1823. *A voyage in the south seas in the years 1812, 1813, and 1814.* London: Sir Richard Phillips.
Pospisil, L. J.
    1958. *Kapauku Papuans and their law.* New Haven: Yale Univ. Press.
    1963. *Kapauku Papuan economy.* New Haven: Yale Univ. Press.
    1967. Legal levels and multiplicity of legal systems in human societies. *Journal of Conflict Resolution* **11**, 2–26.
    1971. *Anthropology of law: A comparative theory.* New Haven: Yale Univ. Press.
    1978. *The ethnology of law,* 2nd edition. Menlo park: Cummings Publishing Co.
Pound, R.
    1942. *Social control through law.* New Haven: Yale Univ. Press.
Procopius.
    550 [1981]. *The secret history.* London: Penguin.
Pulliam, H. R. and Dunford, C.
    1980. *Programmed to learn.* New York: Columbia University Press.
Radcliffe-Brown, A. R.
    1922. *The Andaman islanders.* London: Cambridge.
    1952. *Structure and function in primitive society.* New York: The Free Press.

Rattray, R. S.
   1923. *Ashanti*. Oxford: Clarendon.
   1927. *Religion and art in Ashanti*. Oxford: Clarendon.
   1929. *Ashanti law and constitution*. Oxford: Clarendon.
Reitz, K. P., Dow, M. M., Burton, M. L. and White, D. R.
   1985. AUTCOR and AUTTWO for regression estimates in the presence of one and two autocorrelated disturbances. *World Cultures*, in press.
Reyna, S. P.
   1979. The rationality of divorce: marital instability among the Barma of Chad. *In* G. Kurian, ed. *Cross-cultural perspectives of mate selection and marriage*, pp. 322–341. Westport, Conn.: Greenwood Press.
Reynolds, H.
   1904. Notes on the Azande tribe of the Congo. *African Studies* **3**, 328–346.
Richards, A. I.
   1940. The political system of the Bemba tribe—Northern Rhodesia. *In* M. Fortes and E. E. Evans Pritchard, eds. *African political systems*, pp. 83–120. London: International African Institute.
   1950. Some types of family structure amongst the Central Bantu. *In* A. R. Radcliffe-Brown and D. Forde, eds. *African systems of kinship and marriage*, pp. 83–120. London: Oxford.
Rivers, W. H. R.
   1914. Tikopia. *The history of Melanesian society*, Vol. 1, pp. 298–362. London: Cambridge.
   1924. *Social organization*. New York: Knopf.
Roscoe, J.
   1911. *The Baganda: An account of their native customs and beliefs*. London: Macmillan.
Rowe, J. H.
   1946. Inca culture at the time of the Spanish conquest. *In* J. H. Steward, ed. *Handbook of South American indians*, Vol 2. Washington, D. C.: Government Printing Office.
Saffirio, J., Chagnon, N. A., and Betzig, L. L.
   1982. The use and abuse of Yanomamo kinship terminology (ms.).
Saggs, H. W. F.
   1962. *The greatness that was Babylon*. London: Sidgwick and Jackson.
Sahagun, F. B. de
   1951a. *Florentine codex: General history of the things of New Spain. Book 2, The ceremonies*. Santa Fe: School of American Research.
   1951b. *Florentine codex: General history of the things of New Spain. Book 8, Kings and lords*. Santa Fe: School of American Research.
Sahlins, M. D.
   1958. *Social stratification in Polynesia*. Seattle: University of Washington Press.
   1972. *Stone age economics*. New York: Aldine.
   1976a. *Culture and practical reason*. Chicago: University of Chicago Press.
   1976b. *The use and abuse of biology*. Ann Arbor: Michigan Press.
Salzano, F. J., Neel, J. V. and Maybury-Lewis, D.
   1967. Further studies on the Xavante Indians. *American Journal of Human Genetics* **19**, 463–489.

Sanders, W. T. and Price, B. J.
  1968. *Mesoamerica: The evolution of a civilization.* New York: Random House.
Schapera, I.
  1930. *The Khoisan peoples of South Africa: Bushmen and Hottentots.* London: George Routledge and Sons.
Schebesta, P.
  1928. *Among the forest dwarfs of Malaya.* London: Oxford.
Schultz, T. W.
  1974. Fertility and economic values. *In* T. W. Schultz, eds. *Economics and the family: Marriage, children, and capital,* pp. 3–22. Chicago: University of Chicago Press.
Seligman, C. G. and Seligman, B. Z.
  1932. *Tribes of the Nilotic Sudan.* London: George Routledge and Sons.
Service, E. R.
  1960. The law of evolutionary potential. *In* M. D. Sahlins and E. R. Service, eds. *Evolution and culture,* pp. 93–122. Ann Arbor: University of Michigan Press.
  1962. *Primitive social organization.* New York: Random House.
  1975. *The evolution of the state and civilization.* New York: Norton.
  1978. Classical and modern theories of the origins of government. *In* E. R. Service and R. Cohen, eds. *Origins of the state,* pp. 21–33. Philadelphia: ISHI.
Shepher, J.
  1971. Mate selection among second generation kibbutz adolescents and adults: incest avoidance and negative imprinting. *Archives of Sexual Behavior* **1,** 293–307.
Silk, J. B.
  1980. Adoption and kinship. *American Anthropologist* **82,** 799–820.
Skertchey, J. A.
  1874. *Dahomey as it is.* London: Chapman and Hall.
Slaski, J.
  1950. The Luapula peoples. *In* W. Whiteley, ed. *Bemba and related peoples of northern Rhodesia,* pp. 77–100. London: International African Institute.
Southwold, M.
  1965. The Ganda of Uganda. *In* J. L. Gibbs, ed. *Peoples of Africa,* pp. 81–118. New York: Holt, Rinehart and Winston.
Speke, J. H.
  1864. *Journal of the discovery of the source of the Nile.* New York: Harper and Brothers.
Spencer, H,
  1876 [1967]. *In* R. L. Carneiro, ed. *The evolution of society.* Chicago: University of Chicago Press.
Spencer, W. B. and Gillen, F. J.
  1927. *The Arunta: A study of a stone age people.* London: Macmillan.
Spier, L.
  1930. *Klamath ethnography.* Berkeley: University of California Press.
Spillius, J.
  1959. Natural disaster and population crisis in a Polynesian society: an exploration of operational research. *Human Relations* **10,** 1–27.

Spiro, M. E.
1958. *Children of the kibbutz*. Cambridge: Harvard Univ. Press.

Stair, J. B.
1897. *Old Samoa: or flotsam and jetsam from the Pacific Ocean*. London: The Religious Tract Soceity.

Starr, C. G.
1971. *The ancient Romans*. London: Oxford.

Starr, J. and Yngvesson, B.
1975. Scarcity and disputing: zeroing in on compromise decisions. *American Ethnologist* **2**, 553–566.

Stephens, W. N.
1963. *The family in cross-cultural perspective*. New York: Holt, Rinehart and Winston.

Stern, T.
1965. *The Klamath tribe: A people and their reservation*. Seattle: University of Washington Press.

Stevenson, R. L.
1901. *In the South Seas*. New York: Scribner's Sons.

Stirling, A. P.
1965. *Turkish village*. London: Weidenfeld and Nicolson.

Stout, D. B.
1947. *San Blas Cuna acculturation: An introduction*. New York: Viking Fund.

Strassmann, B. I.
1981. Sexual selection, paternal care, and concealed ovulation in humans. *Ethology and Sociobiology* **2**, 31–40.

Strate, J.
1982. Warfare and political evolution: a cross cultural test. Ph.D. Dissertation, University of Michigan.

Swanton, J. R.
1911. *Indian tribes of the lower Mississippi Valley*. Bureau of American Ethnology, Bulletin 43.

Syme, R.
1960. Bastards in the Roman aristocracy. *Proceedings of the American Philosophical Society* **104**, 323–327.

Symons, D.
1979. *The evolution of human sexuality*. New York: Oxford.

Taylor, D. M.
1946. Kinship and social structure of the Island Carib. *Southwestern Journal of Anthropology* **2**, 180–212.

Terray, E.
1972. *Marxism and "primitive" societies*. New York: Monthly Review.
1975. Classes and class consciousness in the Abron Kingdom of Gyaman. In M. Bloch, ed. *Marxist analyses and social anthropology*, pp. 85–135. New York: Wiley and Sons.

Textor, R. B.
1967. *A cross-cultural summary*. New Haven: HRAF Press.

Thomas, E. M.
1959. *The harmless people*. New York: Vintage Books.

Thompson, R.
1841 [1980]. *The Marquesan Islands*. Laie, Hawaii: Institute for Polynesian Studies.

Thompson, V. M.
1927. *French Indo-China*. New York: Macmillan.

Thornton, A.
1977. Children and marital stability. *Journal of Marriage and the Family*. **39**, 931–940.

Tinbergen, N.
1963. On aims and methods of ethology. *Zeitscrift fur Tierpsychologie* 20, 410-433.

Tocqueville, A. de
1840 [1945]. *Democracy in America*, Vol. 2. New York: Vintage Books.

Toganivalu, D.
1912. Ratu Cakobau. *Transactions of the Fijian Society*, pp. 1–12. Copy at Cumulative Cross Cultural Coding Center, University of Pittsburgh.

Tooker, E.
1964. *An ethnography of the Huron indians, 1615–1649*. Bureau of American Ethnology, Bulletin 190.

Torday, E. and Joyce, T. A.
1906. Notes on the ethnography of the Ba-Yaka. *Journal of the Royal Anthropological Institute*. **36**, 39–58.

Trigger, B. G.
1969. *The Huron*. New York: Holt, Rinehart and Winston.

Trivers, R. L.
1971. The evolution of reciprocal altruism. *Quarterly Review of Biology* **46**, 35–57.
1972. Parental investment and sexual selection. *In* B. Campbell, ed. *Sexual selection and the descent of man*, pp. 136–179. New York: Aldine.

Trivers, R. L. and Willard, D. E.
1973. Natural selection of parental ability to vary the sex ratio of offspring. *Science* **179**, 90–92.

Tuden, A. and Marshall, C.
1972. Political organization: cross-cultural codes 4. *Ethnology* **11**, 436–464.

Turke, P. W.
1984a. On what's not wrong with a Darwinian theory of culture. *American Anthropologist* **86**, 633–638.
1984b. Effects of ovulatory synchrony and concealment on protohominid mating systems and parental roles. *Ethology and Sociobiology* **5**, 33–44.
1984c. Tests of Darwinian and economic theories of fertility determinants on Ifaluk Atoll. Paper read at meetings of the American Anthropological Association, Denver.

Turke, P. W. and Betzig, L. L.
1985. Those who can do: wealth, status, and reproductive success on Ifaluk. *Ethology and Sociobiology* 6, in press.

Turke, P. W. and Irons, W.
In preparation. Population structure and !Kung homicide rates.

Turnbull, C. M.
1965. *Wayward servants: The two worlds of the African pygmies*. Westport, Conn.: Greenwood Press.

Turner, G.
1884. *Samoa, a hundred years ago and long before*. London: Macmillan.
Turner, L. M.
1894. *Ethnology of the Ungava district, Hudson Bay territory*. Bureau of American Ethnology, Bulletin No. 11.
Turrado Moreno, A.
1945. *Ethnography of the Guarauno indians*. Caracas: Lit. y Tip. Vargas. HRAF translation.
Twain, M.
1884 [1958]. *The adventures of Huckleberry Finn*. Boston: Houghton Mifflin.
Tylor, E. B.
1889. On a method of investigating the development of institutions; applied to the laws of marriage and descent. *Journal of the Royal Anthropological Institute*. **18**, 245–269.
United Nations
1977. *Yearbook*. New York: Office of Public Information, United Nations.
Vaillant, G. C.
1941. *Aztecs of Mexico: Origin, rise and fall of the Aztec nation*. Garden City: Doubleday, Doran.
Van den Berghe, P. L.
1979. *Human family systems*. New York: Elsevier.
Van den Berghe, P. L. and Mesher, G.
1980. Royal incest and inclusive fitness. *American Ethnologist* **7**, 300–317.
Van Velzen, H. U. E. T. and Van Wetering, W.
1960. Residence, power groups, and intra-societal aggression. *International Archives of Ethnography* **49**, 169–200.
Vehrencamp, S. L.
1983. A model for the evolution of despotic versus egalitarian societies. *Animal Behavior* **31**, 667–682.
Venable, V.
1945. *Human Nature: The Marxian view*. New York: World Publishing Co.
Veniaminov, I. E. P.
1840. *Notes on the Islands of the Unalaska district*. St. Petersburg: Russian-American Co. HRAF translation.
Verner, J. and Willson, M. F.
1966. The influence of habitats on mating systems of North American passerine birds. *Ecology* **47**, 143–147.
Vlassoff, M.
1982. Economic utility of children and infertility in rural India. *Population Studies* **36**, 45–59.
Vreeland, H. H.
1954. *Mongol community and kinship structure*. New Haven: HRAF Press.
Wade, M. J.
1978. A critical review of the models of group selection. *Quarterly Review of Biology* **53**, 101–114.
Wallis, M. D.
1851 [1967]. *Life in Feejee*. Ridgewood, NJ: Gregg Press.
Waterhouse, J.
1866. *The king and people of Fiji*. London: Wesleyan Conference Office. Copy at Cumulative Cross Cultural Coding Center, University of Pittsburgh.

Watson, J. B.
1952. *Cayuga culture change.* Memoirs of the American Anthropological Association, no. 73.

Weatherhead, P. J. and Robertson, R. J.
1979. Offspring quality and the polygyny threshold: the "sexy son" hypothesis. *American Naturalist* **113**, 201–208.

West Eberhard, M. J.
1967. Foundress associations in polistine wasps: dominance hierarchies and the evolution of social behavior. *Science* **157**, 1584–1585.

1969. The social biology of polistine wasps. *Miscellaneous Publications, Museum of Zoology, University of Michigan,* **140**, 1–101.

1975. The evolution of social behavior by kin selection. *Quarterly Review of Biology* **50**, 1–33.

1978. Temporary queens in *Metapolybia* wasps: non-reproductive helpers without altruism? *Science* **200**, 441–443.

Westermarck, E.
1891. *The history of human marriage.* New York: Macmillan.

White, D. R., Burton, M. L. and Dow, M. M.
1981. Sexual division of labor in African agriculture: a network autocorrelation analysis. *American Anthropologist* **83**, 824–849.

White, L. A.
1949. *The science of culture.* New York: Farrar, Strauss, Giroux.

Whiteley, W.
1950. *Bemba and related peoples of northern Rhodesia.* London: International African Institute.

Whiting, B. B.
1950. *Paiute sorcery.* New York: Viking Fund.

Whiting, J. W. M.
1964. Effects of climate on certain cultural practices. *In* W. H. Goodenough, ed. *Explorations in cultural anthropology* pp. 511–544. New York: McGraw-Hill.

Wilbert, J.
1958. Kinship and social organization of the Yekuana and Goajiro. *Southwestern Journal of Anthropology* **14**, 51–60.

Williams, G. C.
1957. Pleiotropy, natural selection, and the evolution of senescence. *Evolution* **4**, 398–411.

1966. *Adaptation and natural selection: A critique of some current evolutionary thought.* Princeton: Princeton University Press.

1975. *Sex and evolution.* Princeton: Princeton University Press.

Williams, G. C. and Williams, D. C.
1957. Natural selection of individually harmful social adaptations among sibs with special reference to social insects. *Evolution* **11**, 32–39.

Williams, T.
1884. *Fiji and the Fijians.* London: Hodder and Stoughton.

Wilson, D. S.
1980. *The natural selection of populations and communities.* Menlo Park: Benjamin/Cummings.

Wilson, E. D.
1975. *Sociobiology.* Cambridge: Harvard

Wittfogel, K. A.
   1957. *Oriental despotism: A comparative study of total power.* New Haven: Yale Univ. Press.
Woodburn, J.
   1968. Stability and flexibility in Hadza residental groupings. *In* R. B. Lee and I. DeVore, eds. *Man the hunter,* pp. 103–110. New York: Aldine.
Wrangham, R. W.
   1979. On the evolution of ape social systems. *Social Science Information* **18,** 335–368.
   1980. An ecological model of female-bonded primate groups. *Behavior* **75,** 262–300.
   1982. Mutualism, kinship and social evolution. *In* King's College Sociobiology Group, eds. *Current problems in sociobiology,* pp. 269–289. London: Cambridge.
Wrangham, R. W. and Ross, E.
   1983. Lese resources and reproduction. Paper read at Northwestern University.
Wright, S.
   1922. Coefficients of inbreeding and relationship. *American Naturalist* **56,** 330–338.
   1945. Tempo and Mode in Evolution: a critical review. *Ecology* **26,** 414–419.
   1968. *Evolution and the genetics of populations.* Vol. 1. Chicago: University of Chicago Press.
   1980. Genic and organismic selection. *Evolution* **24,** 825–843.

INDEX